"As a teenaged entrepreneur, accomplished athlete, coach, and corporate sales leader, Logan Stout pulled together a cache of dynamic truths which fueled his meteoric success. His new book, Stout Advice, lays out in a clear and accessible way the catalytic principles that readers in various fields can leverage for their own growth and effectiveness!"

-Jim Johnson: Senior Pastor, Preston Trail Community Church

"Being a former professional athlete, all of my success has come from practicing 'the team concept.' Logan's book explains the importance of practicing the team concept in all areas of your life. I have been lucky enough to learn directly from Logan and now you can!"

-Jim Dowd: 17 Year NHL veteran, and Stanley Cup Champion

"In a climate where the goal of many is to achieve success regardless of the damaging cost to themselves and others, Logan Stout is a breath of fresh air. His own success in his life, both personally and professionally, validates the truths he shares in this book. *Stout Advice* will equip the reader to successfully reach lofty goals without stepping off the platform of integrity.

"I heartily recommend *Stout Advice* as a helpful tool for those who want to ascend the stairs to accomplishment. Any group who is fortunate enough to hear Logan Stout speak will be instructed by his knowledge, motivated by his zeal and inspired by a spiritual integrity that is rare."

-Dr. Steve McVey: Author, best selling *Grace Walk*

Stout Advice

The Secrets to building yourself,
people, and teams!

Logan Stout

authorHOUSE®

AuthorHouse™
1663 Liberty Drive
Bloomington, IN 47403
www.authorhouse.com
Phone: 1-800-839-8640

Published by AuthorHouse 11/03/2015

ISBN: 978-1-4817-2027-4 (sc)
ISBN: 978-1-4817-2028-1 (hc)
ISBN: 978-1-4817-2029-8 (e)

Library of Congress Control Number: 2013903598

Printed in the United States of America by BookMasters, Inc
Ashland OH
November 2015

Purpose

The purpose of this book is to communicate in a systematic way how I've been blessed mentally, physically, spiritually, emotionally and relationally in life. Should anything happen to me prematurely, this book is meant to ensure that my twin boys, Miles and Cooper, have these life lessons in print, so they will always know my heart and have the keys to living a blessed life.

Stout Advice is dedicated to Haley, Miles, and Cooper Stout.
They are the loves of my life that I do not deserve.

Acknowledgments

There are many people to thank for the *Stout Advice* project. First and foremost, all blessings come from Him; thank you Jesus! Please continue to enlarge my territory and put me where you want me.

Haley: Thank you for being the most supportive and loving wife and mom. You are the greatest blessing I've ever received, and I will continue to do everything in my power to be the best dad and husband possible.

Miles and Cooper: You two are without question my inspiration and the reason for this book. Should anything ever happen to me, just know this book was written to serve as a road map for your lives. This book flows directly from my heart onto paper and provides the keys to daddy's blessed life.

Family: Dad, Mom, Austin, Gary, Meme, Pete, Grandma, Bamper, uncles, and more, I thank you for all you've done for and with me in this journey called life.

Readers: Thank you for making the time to read and share this book, and I pray it helps you in your success journey.

Motivational, Self-Help, Spiritual, and Leadership authors and leaders: Keep doing what you are doing, as you have impacted my life and many others!

Thank you for reading Stout Advice. We hope the content of this book helps put you on a path to success and life on your own terms. If you'd like to receive more information and insight from Logan and his team of life architects as well as information about speaking events in your area, please visit LoganStout.com.

Table of Contents

Introduction: My Story

My reasons for writing this book are rather simple. First and foremost, no matter where you are in life, the thoughts in this book should resonate with you. This book is for everyone—business owners, coaches, teachers, ministers, parents, athletes, and more. It is for everyone who desires to be the best he or she can be. Most importantly, should anything ever happen to me, I want my two boys, Miles and Cooper, to have something they can look back on to better know their dad. This book reveals the major components that granted me life on my own terms financially by the age of twenty-five, an amazing family, priceless relationships, and the ability to give to those in need.

A lot of people are looking for the key components in life to help them be better at what they do. The information in this book, in my opinion, covers the absolute musts that are required in order to have a high level of success in every facet of life. I have many weaknesses—we all do—but God has given me the ability to not only make millions of dollars but also, more importantly, help others do so as well. He has put it on my heart to write this book as a way of explaining what makes me tick. I pray this information blesses you on your journey toward success, and I hope to meet you soon!

STAGE I of Success: Building You

Chapter 1: It Begins and Ends with You

***Personal development:* a personal commitment
to grow in every area of your life**

I've been extremely blessed to have the ability to live life on my own terms as a result of the growth I've experienced as a person. My goal is for others to experience the same success I've had and more, and I know applying important yet simple principles to life can help people achieve that goal. I spend a lot of time speaking to groups and companies around the world—sometimes groups of thousands—with the primary goal of teaching others how to do what I've done. One of the most common questions I'm asked is "What would you say your number-one key to success has been?" That's a loaded question, but the answer is rather simple: my commitment to personal development. Personal development liberates individuals and allows them to reach their God-given potential in life. The more I've grown as a person, the more successful I've become. The contents of this book will break down the personal development process in detail. Each stage of growth both builds upon and depends on the previous process.

We all have strengths and weaknesses, whether we want to admit it or not. The reality is, everyone knows your weaknesses, so doesn't it make sense for you to know them as well? The process of personal development is a never-ending journey, and it's 100 percent worth it. I've never met a person who regretted personal development. I've also never met a person who didn't wish he or she had started growing earlier in his or her career. It's a classic example of the "if I knew then what I know now" scenario.

The contents of this book come from my lifelong pursuit of personal development. I've found that every facet of our personal development journey both leads us and forms a foundation on which other components may flourish. The first stage in personal development is to know yourself and, thus, believe in yourself.

Belief: unwavering thought of the who or what

Show me someone who truly believes in him or herself, and I'll go to battle with that person any day of the week. We've all had struggles with belief, be it our belief in ourselves, others, ventures, or even God. Let's tap into the key components of belief that ultimately set you free. The feeling that you can rely on yourself or on others is extremely important in order to be successful.

The following story highlights the power of belief.

> The story is told of a Russian schoolboy who had a warm relationship with his father. As an expression of his love, the father would regularly tell the boy, "I'll always be there for you, Son."
>
> Then a day came when the largest earthquake ever to hit Asia struck and crumbled most of the town's buildings to the ground, including the school the boy was attending. For days, the father dug through the rubble, using nothing but his bare hands. He did most of the digging alone, with only an occasional passerby lending aid. "Give it up," said those who saw the desperate father. "He's gone."
>
> But the father held firm to his belief that he would find his son alive. Finally, the father pulled the boy from the wreckage alive, along with several other children from the class who had believed the boy's repeated urgings: "My father will come. Believe me, he will come. He said he will always be there for me, and he will come!" The boy and his friends had stayed alive without food and water for several days, surviving solely on the belief that they would be rescued.

People often say that our beliefs control our actions. The belief we must first instill is the belief in ourselves. Another name for this level of belief is confidence.

Confidence

The googled definition of *confidence* is as follows: "The feeling or belief that one can rely on someone or something; firm trust." To truly believe in yourself, you must truly know yourself. People can't love something they don't truly know; thus, they must love themselves in order to believe in themselves. Now, there's a big difference between confidence and arrogance, and many times really confident people come close to crossing the line. Regardless, I've never seen someone reach big-time success without believing in him or herself. Confidence gives people the ability to overcome the many mental roadblocks in life, thereby allowing them to excel where others fail because they know who they are and where they are going.

Blind Spots

Confidence allows us to be comfortable in our own skin. Put another way: we know who we are and who we aren't when we stay true to ourselves and those around us. The adventure to know yourself allows you to truly get to know your strengths and weaknesses and, thus, gives you the desire to work on both. I don't know anyone who likes being told his or her weaknesses, but I've never met a truly successful person who maintained long-term success without learning to embrace constructive feedback. Pastor and author John Hagee once said, "People would rather be showered with praise that will kill them, versus constructive feedback that will save them." We must find people who will shoot us right between the eyes with constructive feedback.

I do a lot of public speaking, and a friend of mine once asked me if I'd ever listened to myself. At the time, I hadn't—and I had no desire to. Looking back, what he was probably saying was, "You really need to listen to how you come across, because it might not be how you intend to come across." That conversation stuck with me for a while, and then, after reading the quote by Pastor Hagee, I decided to start seeking feedback.

The greatest blessing in my life is my wife, Haley. She's known me since seventh grade and has seen me succeed and fail. I finally built up the courage to ask her for constructive feedback. At first she was hesitant, so I had to literally beg her to hit me between the eyes so that I could improve—and boy did she ever! She finally told me all of the things I so desperately needed to know but had never been open to hearing. Remember this key tip: We all have blind spots. We don't know they exist, but pretty much everyone else does! These blind spots aren't good and need to be corrected. If you are reading this and think blind spots don't apply to you, just remember *why they are called blind spots*: you don't know they exist! Trust me, we all have them, and the sooner you can learn what they are and what you need to do to fix them, the better.

I've been told that one of my greatest strengths is public speaking. I'm asked to speak just about 365 days a year, be it in front of a few hundred people for a small company or in front of ten thousand people in a sold-out arena. If it weren't for my wife and others, I without question wouldn't have all of these requests. I improved my public-speaking skills by 100 percent by simply asking my wife to tell me where I needed to improve. Success-minded people and companies beg for feedback. I can't think of a better example than Apple.

> When it came to big innovations, Jobs did indeed rely on his intuition and imagination. But it is incorrect to assume that Apple never listens to its customers. The exact opposite is true. Apple listens to its customers all the time and, more important, actively solicits feedback from both its internal customers (employees) and external customers.

Apple's mastery of creating surveys and feedback opportunities for their customers was half the equation in their pursuit of success. Applying what they learned from the feedback set them free to fix their blind spots and become one of the most successful companies in the world. Apple's employees display an amazing confidence because they are free to be themselves. Apple stresses the idea of being who God made you to be. Be you! In others words, Apple says, "We believe in you. Be you. Don't be who you think we want you to be. Be comfortable in your own skin—that's all we ask!" Apple creates a culture of confident people. To be successful in life, we must know in our hearts that we ourselves are worthy. In short, we must believe in ourselves.

Belief in Self

Only when we peel back the layers of what the world tells us we should be will we realize who God intended for us to be. I've always believed there are three surefire ways to waste time:

1. Worry a lot
2. Compare yourself to others
3. Be someone you're not

Think about how often we waste time with one or more of the three examples listed above. To combat this, be you. Believe in who you are, not necessarily who everyone wants you to be. If I'd listened to what everyone wanted me to be, I would have been an attorney, an engineer, or something of the like. The only person other than me who truly thought I would play pro baseball was my dad. Everyone else told me all the reasons I wouldn't. All of those same people told me I was crazy when I decided to start my own home-based business. Millions of dollars later, I guess they were wrong. That home-based business has done nearly $6 *billion* in revenue in less than eight years as I write this book. I believed I could play pro baseball for the same reason I believed I could change my life with my start-up business—because I believed in me. And you can believe in yourself too!

You must truly know yourself in order to have the resilient confidence to move mountains. You will find that unwavering confidence is contagious. People are attracted to it. They will believe in you because you believe in you. They will want to know what you are doing so that they don't miss out. Your success will literally breed more success. So where does this unwavering belief originate?

Belief in Your Maker

To know who you are, doesn't it make sense to know who made you? To truly know a car, you should direct any questions about the car to the person who made the vehicle. Consider yourself a vehicle. You have a lot of horsepower that was inserted into your being from birth. How do you capitalize on the unique horsepower given to you? Get to know your Maker!

Jim Johnson, pastor of Preston Trail Community Church, states, "If we are made in the image of God, then locked inside the heart of every person is the potential to be an innovator, an initiator, and an influencer. That is, a leader. If God is the designer of all things and is good, it makes the most sense to follow his principles for life. When we follow his life directions, marriages, families, organizations, companies, and even churches just work better!

We were all put onto this earth by God's design. He wants nothing but the best for us, but it's up to us to use the gifts He's given us to the fullest. If you think He just gives you what you want, you are wrong. God is not a genie in a bottle or a good-luck charm. He is your Creator, not your dictator. He allows us to freely choose the paths we want to go down. Without getting into a theological debate on predestination and the like, I'm simply saying that if you want something, go get it. We have been inundated with the lottery mind-set. People think success happens overnight. It doesn't.

Success happens by doing the right things repeatedly over an extended period of time. We must embrace the reality that success is neither a marathon nor a sprint. It's both! Success takes time, and to truly be successful, we must allow the Holy Spirit to guide our paths. So often we either go ahead of the Holy Spirit or lag behind. Be one with your Maker, and the Holy Spirit will give you clarity as to the direction you should go.

God, Jesus, and the Holy Spirit

I'm reminded of the "Footprints in the Sand" prayer from my youth.

The poem is about an individual who dreams he is walking on the beach, and he sees his life reflected in a series of visions in the sky. As these visions flash across the sky, the individual notices there is only one set of footprints during the most difficult times of his life, and two sets of footprints appear during the easiest times in his life. The individual is bothered because the Lord had promised He would always be there, yet it seems in the dream that the Lord abandoned the individual during the difficult times, thus the reason for the single set of footprints during those scenes. The individual proceeds to confront the Lord about the issue, asking why His promise to always be there was not fulfilled. The Lord replies, "I would never, never leave you during your times of trial and suffering. When you saw only one set of footprints, it was then that I carried you."

One of my daily prayers is to seek God's will in my life. In other words, I want to spend each second of the day pursuing what God desires for me to pursue. It's easy to pursue our own motives and initiatives, but it's a whole lot easier when we wait on the Holy Spirit to prompt us and push us in the right direction. More often than not, we wait until we are already in a bind before we ask for God's assistance. Instead, we should seek his will in our lives every day—*before* we get into trouble. I'm reminded of Matthew 7:7: "Ask and it will be given to you; seek and you will find; knock and the door will be opened to you." It's easy to forget the role our Maker has in our daily lives. This world can be a lonely place if you go at it alone. Have the belief that your Maker is not only there for you at all times but also guiding you if you simply call on Him. Until people truly know their Maker, they will always have the feeling that something is missing in life. Money, cars, homes, and even people are temporal. They come and go. There is only one constant we have to hold on to: our heavenly Father. Once we understand Him, we will understand ourselves, and our hearts will begin to focus on the eternal. Don't get me wrong—I like having nice things. But I've never seen someone's earthly possessions at his or her funeral. The person presiding over the funeral doesn't say, "Here lies John Doe and all of his stuff." When your time is up, what are people going to say about you? I sure hope people say a lot more than "He sure had nice things." There's nothing wrong with dabbling in the temporal as long as we live for the eternal. Once our hearts are focused on the eternal, we then begin to see things more clearly. Most importantly, we begin to see why we are here. This change in perspective not only gives us confidence but also helps us see the greatness in everyone. We begin to see what success looks like in others. Our belief in our Maker literally fuels our belief in ourselves and in others. It's this unwavering belief that gives us the momentum to get moving and take action. We see the opportunities that ordinarily would pass us by. We have clear vision!

Chapter Summary:

1. What's your level of belief in yourself?
2. Do you have a daily game plan to grow in your faith?

3. Do you maintain an eternal perspective, or are you focused on the temporal?
4. Do you have a personal relationship with your Maker?
5. Do you pray through every decision, or do you wait until you are already in a bind?

Chapter 2: See What No One Sees

Vision: the ability to see things others don't

Belief expands vision. Once we understand the importance of belief on the success journey, we must realize the role vision plays in putting our belief into action. Success must first happen in our minds before we ever take the chance to act. Our confidence grows as a result of our exploration into the depths of our soul, so it's important to understand the role of vision.

It's been said one can't escape his or her own perspective, and I fully agree. Put another way, we all see life through our own set of lenses, thereby influencing our views, or perspective, of what we see and how we see it. Some call this our worldview. A worldview is oftentimes thrown upon us by parents, relatives, friends, and the environment we are born into, and those factors certainly influence the way we live life. If we aren't in tune with the past and present influences that ultimately determine the way we live life, our vision is cloudy. In order to have clear vision, we must understand what shapes our worldview—and what shapes the worldviews of those around us. Vision enables us to progress with all of the moving components of life in a focused direction, thereby attaining clarity and direction in a confusing, fast-paced world while never losing track of why we started our particular journey in the first place. It's probably safe to say you are reading this book to aid you in your success journey. You want the vision, so to speak, so you can take your life to the next level. This is exactly what I wanted when I started my success journey, and I still do to this day. It's a continuous journey.

Upbringing

At this point, it's important to stop surging ahead and instead pause and think about your upbringing. Why are you the way you are? Why did you pursue the things you did? The answers to these questions will give you the starting point you need to clarify why you are where you are so that you can be where you want to be. If you project two, five, even ten years down the road, assuming nothing changes in your life, where are you going to be? Where do you want to be? If you can do anything, anywhere, with anyone, what does that picture look like? To have the vision of where we want to be is a step in the right direction, but we must first look at where we are and reflect on why we are who we are. Chances are, to be where you want to be, you are going to need to change some things, and that starts with you.

My parents were good about allowing me to carve my own path in the world. They never forced me to play sports or an instrument per se, but looking back, I realize that their influence played a key role in what I chose to pursue. My dad always says, "We never forced sports on Logan; we were going to support him in whatever it was he chose to do." Looking back, although he may not have forced sports on me, I would say buying me youth basketball goals, baseball gloves, footballs, and more certainly qualifies as praying I would like sports. For the record, I'm grateful he encouraged me to love sports, and I plan on doing the same for my twin boys. I can't remember a single family moment that didn't involve watching Sunday afternoon basketball at the Stout household. My grandfather sat in one recliner, and my grandmother sat in the other. My dad and his four brothers piled into every open chair they could. I would sit two feet in front of the television, watching Magic Johnson and Larry Bird go at it! It was awesome. At halftime, I would go into the backyard and replay the first half, including Magic Johnson's no-look pass off the wall, hook shot and all. Then Bird would drain a three-pointer from the corner. Stinky and sweaty, I would run back in before the second half started so as not to miss a single play. Without a doubt, my dad and his brothers would get into competitive arguments about anything and everything possible. The jockeying match would start with the game we were all watching and then quickly turn to baseball, football, and everything else they could think of to butt heads about. Heck, on more than one occasion, fights ensued. Looking back, I can't imagine why I'm so competitive and stubborn. I was right in the middle of the most competitive and stubborn family on the block. Don't get me wrong—I'm not complaining at all. It's quite the opposite. I am who I am because of those experiences. You don't get to the top by being passive and unopinionated. *You have to stand for something in life or you won't go anywhere. I've never seen a sitting person outrun a standing person.* Those Sunday afternoons with the Stout family influenced who I am today. I learned a lot of what to do and say, and I learned a lot about what not to do and say. My worldview was formed early on; I learned to play sports, be bold, voice my ideas, and fight for what I believe in. The Stout family didn't teach me these traits intentionally. They didn't say to each other, "Let's stage arguments every Sunday afternoon so that Logan can see what it means to have a well-thought-out idea, communicate effectively, and justify why he believes what he believes."

My mom's side of the family had their fare share of memorable moments as well. My parents divorced when I was fairly young, so I spent a lot of time with my mom and her parents. My mom's dad, Pete, taught me more about negotiations and sales than any book ever could have. If there was a way to make an extra buck, we were on it. Every day after school, my little brother and I walked over to Pete's house to grab an afternoon snack and check on his latest boat project. He always had boats in the backyard, as he loved to buy used boats, fix them up, and then sell them. As my grandmother always said, "One man's junk is another man's treasure." Pete would take a boat the entire world had given up on and turn it into a profitable beauty. He had great vision! He knew exactly what each boat was and, most importantly, what it could become. That's what proper vision can do for all of us! I watched my grandfather close boat deal after boat deal, and none of them were executed the same way, but they all had one of two outcomes. Either he would get what he wanted for his boat, or he would literally run the victim off his yard because the offer was too low!

On one particular afternoon, when my brother and I strolled into the backyard, instead of working on a boat, he had a bunch of trash bags, keys in his hand, and a big grin on his face. He said, "Boys, there's a new way to help the earth and make money called recycling." I was about ten years old at the time, and my brother was about seven or so; we had never really heard of recycling, but my grandfather had found a way to make a buck—literally. My brother and I jumped into the pickup, and off we went. We pulled up next to a Dumpster, and my grandfather said, "All right, boys, here we go. It's time to make some money!" At this point, my brother and I had no clue how we were going to make money with some trash bags and a Dumpster. This recycling thing was really confusing. Then came the orders: "Logan, you and I are going to throw Austin into the Dumpster. Austin will grab all of the aluminum cans he can find and throw them in these garbage bags, and then we will head to the next Dumpster. We will make money on every can we find by turning them in to the recycling bin at the end of the day. Now, whatever you boys do, don't tell your momma about this, ya hear?" Long story short, we had more bags of cans than we could count. His entire truck bed was packed, and we held more bags in our laps. We sang all the way to the bank! We pulled up to the drop-off point so that we could cash in our cans. While Pete was inside, my brother and I couldn't wait to see how much we'd made. We were thinking of all the things we were going to buy with all of our hard-earned profits! On a sidenote, you should have smelled my brother. I think we were all drunk from the smell of beer oozing off of his clothes. Pete always said, "You gotta work hard before you get to play hard." The way my brother smelled had me wondering if recycling was worth it. A few moments later, we saw Pete coming out of the building, and his smile was gone. He opened the door, started the truck and started driving home. My brother and I immediately knew the outcome hadn't been as profitable as we had thought, but we were dying to know what we'd earned. Right before I could ask the obvious question, Pete said, "Well, boys, let's chalk this up to a good learning experience. You win some, and you lose some, but you will never win if you don't try." This time we'd tried and lost, but we certainly learned to stay the heck out of Dumpsters! "Just remember, don't tell your momma, because that will be a lot worse than the five dollars we made digging through Dumpsters all day!"

Needless to say, my work ethic and entrepreneurship were certainly influenced by Pete. He encouraged me to try everything possible to make money as long as it was morally and ethically sound. I went door-to-door selling drawings, crossword puzzles, and anything else I could put on a piece of paper. I had a garage sale in his backyard just about every month (digging through Dumpsters can pay off), set up lemonade stands, cleaned windows, and of course mowed yards. From an early age, I learned to seek what I wanted and find opportunities by solving people's problems. Just as important, all these endeavors taught me how to handle objections and rejections, and to use those moments to fuel my fire, not squelch it. In other words, never allow people or situations to keep you from what you set out to do. Keep the vision!

These experiences made me who I am today. We cannot escape our past; we can simply acknowledge it and learn from it. I have a lot of great qualities as a result of my past, and I also have a lot of weaknesses that I constantly work on to rid myself of. Our past experiences, environments, and upbringing form the way we see the world today. Think about religion. Why do people choose to be Baptist, Catholic, Mormon, Methodist, or any other denomination? Most often, they don't choose. They simply plug in to the same denomination their parents raised them in. As time takes its course, people may change the way they see the world due to the current environment, experiences, and influences in their lives. Typically speaking, very few ever stop and question why they go to the particular church they go to. Our worldview, or perspective, comes from our past and our current existence. For example, if you or I see an overweight, gray-haired man with a beard, we think nothing of it. If a three-year-old sees the same man, you may get a "Mommy and Daddy, look! It's Santa Claus!" Bottom line: your way of seeing the world is influenced by a lot of factors. Therefore, pay attention to who or what you surround yourself with at all times before you become someone God never intended you to be! In order to have clear vision, we must pay attention to what we hear, watch, and read, and whom we hang around. My family had a major impact on why I see the world the way I do. I bet yours did as well!

Mind-Set

Picture your mind as a perfect little island sitting in the middle of crystal-clear blue water. Day one of your life, you are prefect. You don't know how to steal, cheat, curse, manipulate, or perform any other bad behavior you can think of.

Everything about the water and the beach is perfect. As time goes on, your brain becomes inundated with the world, and your once-perfect beach becomes cluttered with so much junk that you can barely see the sand. Negativity, sin, discouragement, resentment, jealousy, lies, and every other negative vice or form of moral depravity you can think of pile into your brain. Heck, it's nearly impossible to watch television without half-naked people being thrown at you! Let's face it: we all like to see that sort of stuff, but it corrupts our worldview to the point where we become numb to it—and even crave more. If the perfect beach has only one piece of trash on it, that trash stands out like a sore thumb. However, when the beach isn't cleaned regularly, more and more trash ruins the once-perfect beach, and trash becomes the norm. The human mind functions the same way. We must keep our minds clean and clear of the clutter, or else we will become numb, and our vision will constantly get cloudier without us even realizing it.

This illustration paints the perfect picture of clear and clouded vision. To think clearly, you must keep your mind as spotless as possible. A spotless mind gives you clarity to see right from wrong, good from bad, and where to focus your energies and efforts versus where to stop pursuing a project. There's no reason to run with blinders on when God has given you the ability to see with clear vision, but it takes a continuous renewal of our minds and vision.

Iron Sharpens Iron

The quickest way to get off the success highway is to surround yourself with the wrong people. We've all been around negative influences in our lives. These individuals may be fun to be with, but they will distract you from reaching your God-given potential! Perhaps they like to have a little too much fun and overindulge. Perhaps they bring unsavory conversations to the table. We all like to have these kinds of friends/acquaintances around, but that doesn't mean we should! Success comes from staying focused on the vision, and to do so, we must eliminate as many distractions as possible. Don't get me wrong—it's important to have a good time and vacate, so to speak, into meaningless conversations and activities. However, as with anything in life, moderation is crucial. For example, you have to have water to survive, yet when we drink too much water, we die.

The negative influences I'm referencing are people and conversations that bring you down. If you are wondering whether a person qualifies as a negative person, ask yourself this simple question: "When this person calls me, do I look forward to the phone call, or do I pray he or she doesn't leave a message?" If you see the person's name on the caller ID and every part of you wants to avoid answering the call, you probably need to fire that individual from your life. You can spend only a certain amount of energy in a day, and you don't want to waste any of your valuable energy on people who drain your battery. God has blessed you with a lot of horsepower and a fully charged battery, but if you forget to turn the interior light off, your battery will eventually die. Negative people cause us to continually think about stuff we don't need to waste our time thinking about. Therefore, our brains work overtime, thus keeping our light on and draining our battery. You are a perfectly built vehicle, and God has set you up to succeed. Don't allow others to limit your ability. Negative people get you off course and cause you to take your eyes off the ball. Stay focused on the vision! Successful people understand the reality of peaks and valleys in anything worthwhile. Expect them.

Peaks and Valleys

Life is full of peaks and valleys, so our ability to stay focused and overcome the tough times requires clear vision.

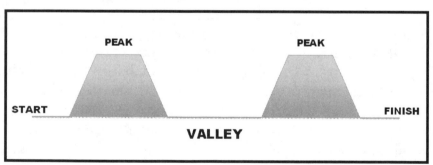

To go from one peak to the next, you must realize that a valley does in fact exist. There's no such thing as the perfect business, relationship, or long-term experience. There will be struggles along the way, and quite frankly, those struggles are what make the journey worth it. Struggles enable us to appreciate what we are fighting for. Think of it this way: the only reason you appreciate a warm shower is because you have had a cold shower. If you'd never had a cold shower, you wouldn't know the difference. If accomplishing success in any particular endeavor were easy, you wouldn't appreciate the accomplishment. It would simply be an activity. In order to fight through the difficulties in life, we must never lose sight of why we started the journey in the first place. Vision gives us the hope to keep fighting for what we want. The vision of what *can be* keeps us in the game. It's when we can no longer see the light at the end of the tunnel that we stop fighting and die. Vision reminds us of what can be, what we are hoping for.

Hope

Victor Frankl's experience, as dictated in his book *Man's Search for Meaning*, illustrates a remarkable example of the power of hope. Frankl witnessed firsthand those who lost the vision and those who maintained the vision of freedom. One of the primary keys to his success was hope. Frankl survived the Nazi prison camps despite the fact that the majority of prisoners died. Hope is the catalyst for perseverance. We choose to keep going because we still have hope for a positive outcome.

Frankl says, "Those who have a 'why' to live, can bear with almost any 'how.'" Frankl's vision literally kept him alive while the majority died in the prison camps. Think about Frankl's story in relation to your own life. How can you apply the life lesson of vision and hope from Victor Frankl to your current situation? Perhaps you started a business venture and are struggling to get through the valley—keep going! Maybe you are in a marriage or a relationship that has fallen on hard times—never lose the vision of why you entered into the relationship. Never quit, as you might be one breakthrough away from reaching the other peak!

Perseverance

If you are willing to simply fail long enough at something, you might just be successful one day! Remember, a failure is an event, not a person. You only fail when you stop getting up. Successful people aren't necessarily gifted; rather, they simply won't quit! I believe Zig Ziglar quoted something to the effect of "There's no such thing as a smooth mountain, because if there were, how in the world would you climb it?" The ruts are necessary to boost us up to the next level in life.

Consider your life as a bunch of chapters. During the transitional times in our lives, one chapter ends and the next one begins. We should learn from each chapter but never stay there. When we live in the past, we mess up the here and now. All of the pages in the past are written and done, but the pages staring you in the face are blank, so cherish every second and make each chapter better than the previous one. In most books, some chapters are tough and even difficult. The hero might struggle through horrifying times, but there's always that next chapter. The hero never stops in the middle of a chapter; he or she keeps going! At the end of the book, the hero prevails and gets what he or she wants, and everyone lives happily ever after. You are the hero in your own book, so keep plugging along. I've never met any truly successful people who didn't go through tough times to get where they are. The key to their success was that they never quit. They had the discipline to stick and stay. They had a plan and worked it diligently until they achieved the results they were looking for.

Vision keeps us locked in on the big picture, and hope fuels us to persevere despite the fact that we can't always see how we are going to accomplish the vision we originally had. Consider perseverance the daily grind of life that enables us to reach the next chapter.

Just about every relationship or venture in life starts with a peak and ends with a peak as long as you stick with it, but there will inevitably be a valley in the middle. For example, think back to your first real relationship. Remember how stupid in love you were? Phone calls would last hours and hours, and at the end of the call, each of you would take turns saying, "You hang up," followed by "No, you hang up," and so on. Then, when someone finally hung up, the other person would call back and say, "Why did you hang up?" As time went on, the relationship matured, and your phone calls likely lasted about thirty seconds. Relationships all start off exciting and passionate and blah blah blah. When all of the puppy love wears off, then—and only then—do you see what the relationship is really all about. Arguments and disagreements take place, and then you realize your partner does actually have some flaws, but you learn to love your partner unconditionally. At that point, you have entered into the valley. As long as you remember why you fell in love with that person in the first place, you can grow old together and learn to love life until you eventually reach the other peak. You will find yourselves celebrating twenty-five years of marriage instead of facing divorce. Through sickness and health and the ups and downs of life, we persevere. Life is full of unexpected peaks and valleys, but the combination of perseverance, hope, and vision propels us from peak to peak.

Vision enables us to see a project through to the end. Put another way: we stay committed. One's level of commitment is directly related to one's level of belief. Vision keeps you in the game, and the longer you are in the game, the easier it is to reach the final pitch! Vision, hope, and perseverance fuel our courage, which leads us to do what few will.

Chapter Summary:

1. Have a clearly defined vision of where you want to be twelve, twenty-four, and sixty months from today. Write this down in a place where you will see it and be reminded of it daily (perhaps on your bathroom mirror, computer screen saver, or cell-phone backdrop).
2. If nothing changes in your life, where are you going to be in twelve, twenty-four, or sixty months? Where do you want to be?
3. What steps or actions must you take, and what changes must you make, to see your vision come to fruition?
4. Write down the significant facets of your life (marriage, relationships, work, etc.) and apply the previous three questions to those areas.
5. Reflect on peaks and valleys in your life and consider how vision, hope, and perseverance fueled you to success.

Chapter 3: Do What No One Will

Courage: seizing opportunities when very few do

Belief gives us the mind-set to see success. Vision, perseverance, the ability to embrace adversity, and hope give us the courage to take action. The best example of courage I can think of is depicted beautifully in Andy Stanley's book _Next Generation Leader_, in which he describes the courage David displayed when he took down Goliath. As Stanley writes, "Leaders understand the unique roles of confidence and caution. Courage requires both. David's caution did not keep him from battle, but neither did he allow his confidence to blind him to the need to select his stones with care." No one wanted to fight Goliath except David. David's willingness to seize the moment elevated him to the status of king. Courage enables us to seize an opportunity that others won't.

Courage is, without question, a necessity if you want to reach success. We must take action to succeed, and courage fuels action. The other essential qualities of success we've discussed certainly build courage. It's pretty hard to move forward if we don't believe we can accomplish the end result. We must first believe we can succeed before we move forward, but belief isn't enough. We must take action, and courage is the ingredient essential to seizing the moment.

The road to success is never clearly defined on day one. We must have the courage to keep going until the goal is in sight. Then—and only then—will we have a clear picture of the path toward success. The hardest phase of just about any venture, business, or movement is getting started. Initial problems might include raising capital, hiring the right people, firing the wrong people that you just hired, controlling inventory, finding customers, having those customers come back, and more. Once your company surpasses the start-up stage, the road to success typically becomes a little more defined. Many times, people get caught up in the *how* instead of focusing on *what* needs to be done. Many incredible people never take advantage of their great ideas, because they are paralyzed by the *how*. Andy Stanley says, "The fact that *how* is challenging is the very reason it provides you with great opportunity … If the pathway into the future were well lit, it would be crowded. If *how* wasn't a problem, somebody else would have already figured it out." What's the solution? Courage! Have the courage to get started. When you focus on *what* you are trying to accomplish, *how* to get it done will become clearer. I'm not saying you shouldn't plan your work before you work your plan. The sad truth is that many people have succeeded with amazing business ideas that weren't even their own ideas. Some people simply get paralyzed from day one on the *how*, while others have the courage to get started.

Think about golf. Even those of you who can't stand the thought of golf still understand the point of the game: put the ball in the hole! The movie *Happy Gilmore* illustrates the *what*-versus-*how* concept perfectly. Happy Gilmore, played by Adam Sandler, has the craziest golf swing ever. His background is in hockey; thus, he hits a golf ball the same way he would a hockey puck. When experts try to change his swing, he says something to the effect of "Just let me put the ball in hole."

I recall hearing golf commentators say that Bubba Watson, the 2012 Masters champion, never took golf lessons. He has a very unorthodox swing, but he won the biggest golf event of the year. He gets to wear the green jacket because he wasn't worried about the *how* (what he looks like); he was focused on the *what* (putting the ball in the hole in as few strokes as possible). Bubba Watson has the courage to go against the grain—a courage that comes from fully believing in who he is and what he's doing. Let me be clear: I believe in the value of private lessons in the various sports of the world. Bubba Watson is the exception and certainly not the rule. I personally think it's crazy not to get private lessons, and who knows just how good Bubba Watson would be if he'd actually had lessons growing up. However, the fact still remains that his belief in himself, along with his courage to take action on that belief, earned him a win at the 2012 Masters.

Leaders are decisive. They make decisions quickly and boldly. Courage allows this action. The ability to quickly gather important information and make a decision often eludes the most talented of people, thereby putting a lid on their overall abilities. What is it exactly that enables some individuals to be decisive, while others aren't? Courage.

Take two guys, for instance. Guy 1 and Guy 2 are both eyeing the same young lady. Guy 1 immediately starts to think about *how* he's going to start the conversation. He starts contemplating all of the possible pickup lines or icebreakers he can use. He then remembers the last time he asked a girl out and the outcome wasn't favorable. Negative thoughts start pouring into Guy 1's head. In the meantime, Guy 2 simply walks over to the young lady and says hello. Over an hour later, Guy 1 is tired of watching Guy 2 and the young lady laugh and carry on, so he decides to leave. In this scenario, Guy 2 was focused on *what* he wanted and not on *how* he was going to go about it.

Courageous leaders aren't without fear; they simply consider and quickly overcome fear. Guy 2 had been turned down before. He'd gone after things in life that hadn't turned out well, but the lessons he'd learned from his failed attempts were a lot less painful than the lesson Guy 1 learned in this scenario: you will miss 100 percent of the opportunities you don't pursue! Guy 1 had the paralysis-by-analysis disease. Not only was he stuck on the *how*, but he also wandered into the worst-case-scenario mind-set and got stuck there, dwelling on the negative. Meanwhile, Guy2 thought about the worst-case scenario and quickly tuned it out. He figured, *I don't have the girl now, so if she turns me down after I ask, I'm in the same place. If she says yes, then I've gained, and I've lost nothing!* Courageous thinkers consider all possible outcomes but never stop moving forward.

It's hard to move forward without action, and courage keeps you moving in a positive direction. We must never underestimate the power of our actions.

High school was an amazing time in my life. I had great friends, a blessed sports experience, and wonderful memories. One of my greatest memories is Young Life. For those who don't know, YL is a unique approach to reaching youth for the kingdom of God. At first I denied the constant invites from Brian Summerall, the YL leader at the time, but after a year or so, I finally went. Attending YL on Monday nights at 7:29 became a regular event for me. It was unlike anything I had ever attended and, quite frankly, wasn't anything like I'd thought it would be. All are welcome to attend YL, regardless of their belief system, denomination, and the like. I was one of those kids who knew of God but didn't really understand anything about Christianity. The funny thing is, I originally went to YL only because everyone else was going, and of course I wanted to get Brian Summerall off my back. I had no idea the impact Brian Summerall would have on my life. He wasn't pushy about inviting me; he simply related to me and consistently reminded me that YL was taking place. The message I received at YL ultimately led me on a faith journey that changed my life. The craziest part about what you just read is that, at the time, I never told Brian! It wasn't until a decade after high school that I finally told Brian about the impact he'd had on my life. The power of his actions was completely unknown to him, yet it changed my life and the lives of thousands of others. I constantly remind myself and others of the courage and actions of Brian Summerall, as we may never know the impact we have on an individual's life.

Actions lead to results! We must never underestimate the power of what we both do and don't do. Courage gives us the responsibility of owning the outcomes and consequences of our actions. Too many times, we get caught up in making excuses. As the founder and CEO of the Dallas Patriots Baseball Organization and Premier Baseball Academies, I'm fortunate to be around a lot of parents and kids. The one major problem I see brewing within society as a whole is the excuse mind-set. People don't own the results. They want to make excuses for anything and everything that doesn't go exactly their way. If my boys have the lowest batting averages on the team, we are going to own that issue. We aren't going make excuses as to why the results are what they are. The bottom line is this: they are what they are. We must be solution-oriented and eliminate any and all excuses. I wouldn't expect my boys to be in the starting lineup until their hitting improves. Instead, parents start blaming the coach, the bat, the umpire, and pretty much anything else you can think of. I even had one parent quit a team because his son was hitting fifth in the lineup and not fourth; the parent claimed that's why he wasn't able to perform as well. If he had been hitting one spot higher in the lineup, he would have performed a lot better. This is a victim mind-set, not a courageous mind-set. Excuses will never get us where we want to be in life. We must own our results. I was always told to perform in the manner of the job or role that I one day wished to have. In other words, if I wanted to be the starting shortstop, for example, then I had to show everyone why I should be the starting shortstop. Don't bad-mouth others or make excuses as to why someone else is in a role you want to be in.

In the business world, I hear people attribute success to luck. Jim Collins, author of *Good to Great, Great by Choice* and many other books, responds with "What's your return on luck?" In other words, even if you believe luck plays a role in success, be it good luck or bad luck, you still have to take action on the lucky circumstance you've been afforded. Simply being lucky doesn't lead to success without action. To say someone reached a certain level of success only by luck is simply an excuse. You can make success stories, or you can make excuses, but you can't make both. Avoid the excuse mind-set at all costs. If you stay courageous in your thinking, great things will happen!

Courage motivates us to act and keeps us moving in the right direction. It acts as a catalyst and also operates like inertia. Furthermore, courage keeps us thinking in a positive and progressive manner. A successful person avoids finger-pointing, excuse making, and the like as much as humanly possible. A courageous leader instead seeks and finds opportunities while everyone else complains and looks for what's wrong. The former says, "Let's find a way to get it done," while the latter says, "It can't be done." A courageous person's mind-set is action-oriented, while a victim's mind-set is based on thoughts without action.

Courage Mind-Set	*Victim Mind-Set*
I will.	They stopped me.
It's my fault.	It's their fault.
Let's find a way.	There is no way.

Author and leader Jim Rohn said, "The day you graduate from childhood to adulthood is the day you take full responsibility for your life." Many people read great books, listen to amazing motivational speakers, and take great notes, but very few actually take action on what they learn. They end up having a bunch of great knowledge but no results. Courage is the catalyst to spur you into action so that you can have the life God desires for you. The component of discipline directs your courage.

Chapter Summary:

1. What opportunities should you pursue?
2. Are you a *what* or a *how* thinker?
3. Check your mind-set: courageous or victim?

Chapter 4: Stay the Course

***Discipline:* to plan your work and work your plan repeatedly over an extended period of time**

Just about everyone wants the same things: money, freedom, more family time, a better lifestyle, or simply the ability to give abundantly. However, few have the discipline to achieve their dreams. Of those who see a great opportunity, only a small percentage have the discipline to stick with it. Many people face a little adversity, get distracted, and quit. There are a few absolutes required in order to have the discipline it takes to be who God created you to be.

Consistency

Does what you say, think, and do align? Are you consistent in every aspect of your life? Would the people you live with and the people you work with view you the same way? Many people live different lives. We all wear different hats, so to speak, because we all get pulled in different directions. For example, perhaps during one part of the day you have to play parent and then spouse—or both at the same time. Then you have to play boss and then answer to your boss, and after work, you may have other social circles you run in. One of the keys to success is to be consistent in conduct and conversation regardless of whom you are with or where you are.

I can't even begin to tell you how many times I thought I knew someone and then, after he got a few drinks in him on about hole 10, felt as if I never knew him. Don't get me wrong—it's great to let loose and have some fun at times. That's not what I'm referencing. I'm referring to the people who live the Las Vegas lifestyle: "what happens in Vegas stays in Vegas." For example, some men act as if they are the perfect husbands in front of their wives, and at other times, you would bet they weren't even married. This duplicity isn't how life works for those who desire to reach their God-given potential in life. We must be the same person regardless of the circumstances. It takes extreme discipline to stay consistent in life as the world throws all types of distractions our way. The ability to stay on course and do the right things over and over again ultimately decides your outcome, and discipline is the key to consistency.

The Lottery Mind-Set

The lottery mind-set has corrupted our society. People think success comes from some big aha moment, when nothing could be further from the truth. Most people want to have success yesterday, so they cut corners every way possible and end up running in circles. There are no shortcuts. The saying "The only place where success comes before work is in the dictionary" hits the nail on the head. Just about every time I speak, someone comes up to me afterward and asks me, "What's the number-one key to success?" My response usually varies, depending on the topic I just spoke about, but I always want to say the same thing: there isn't just one key and never will be, so stop looking for the shortcut! Regardless of your goal, there will be a process to follow in order to become the best possible version of you. Whether your goal is to be the best parent or spouse, employee or boss, family member or friend, you will have to follow a process, and you must maintain discipline. No one simply arrives at being the best of the best. It's a never-ending process of discipline not only to arrive at the top but also to stay there. Regardless of what you do in life, you are either getting better or getting worse. There's no such thing as staying stagnant. Master the principle of doing something every day to improve.

Goal Setting

Goal setting is a must for anyone who truly wishes to hit the success bull's-eye. Let's face it—you can't hit something you can't see. Therefore, we must have clearly defined goals that build upon each other, and we must make them visible. To simply have a goal isn't enough. Our goals should be results-oriented, based on the "control what you can control" mind-set. For instance, one of the goals for your company might be to have $100,000 in partnership revenue for the year. That's a lofty goal, so you must set action-oriented goals to help you achieve your primary goal.

Goal-Setting Example

Primary Goal: Gain $100,000 in partnership revenue.

Action Goals: Make five phone calls per week, accomplish two actual quality meetings per week, and detail each and every outcome of such meetings and calls.

The action goals are what we can control. We can't control the outcomes of the meetings, but we can figure that if we have the proper action goals, they will equate to the primary goal we set out to accomplish. Too many times, we either don't set a goal at all, or we don't have actions lined up to hit the primary goal we hope for.

Let's use the example of wanting to be the best spouse possible. We will assume you have certain responsibilities in your relationship; thus, the following example may apply.

Primary Goal: Be the best husband possible.

Action Goals: I will set aside every Friday night from 6:00 p.m. to 10:00 p.m. for date night. I will book the reservations, etc. I will make sure I keep everything clean, take out the trash, etc. (whatever it is you and your spouse have agreed upon from day one). I will make sure I tell my wife how much I love her and will make sure she is the first person/thing I acknowledge the second I come home every day. I will be more patient and make sure to listen before speaking.

Hopefully you get the point! I used to write my goals on my mirror, so I was reminded of them every morning when I woke up and every night before I went to bed. I encourage you to do the same thing. Goals are valuable only if we remember them on a regular basis.

And 1 Principle

The And 1 Principle simply means to do one more than you originally set out to do. If you are in the gym, do one more rep. If you are in sales, make one more phone call per week. The And 1 Principle is a simple concept, but most people don't have the discipline to do what they originally set out to do, let alone add the And 1 Principle to the equation. In the world of the lottery mind-set, people want instant satisfaction and results. If it's going to take too long to get what they want, they start spending a lot of time looking for a shortcut. In the amount of time they spend trying to cut corners, they likely could have accomplished the end result they originally set out to conquer. Have the discipline to carry out your action-oriented goals, and simply add one to the goal. If you normally do ten reps, do eleven. If you run for twenty minutes a day, run for twenty-five. If you do ten recruiting calls a day, do eleven. Make a point to do a little more each day, and watch it add up!

If you've ever watched a baseball game, you may have noticed that in between innings, the infielders take ground balls on the infield while the pitcher gets loose. The first baseman rolls ground balls to each infielder to help him stay loose. I challenge all of our players with the Dallas Patriots to get an extra ground ball in by getting back out to their positions as quickly as possible in between innings. If they can get an extra 5 ground balls in a game, times 70 games, that's an extra 350 ground balls of practice they would not have had otherwise. Little things add up to big things, and that's exactly how success comes about! With a balanced life, we can implement the And 1 Principle.

Balance

Many people have workout and work-related goals, but few have relational goals. We must have discipline in every facet of our lives. Too many times, we focus on the things that provide tangible results (lost weight, more income, etc.); thus, the people who are most important to us get all of our leftover time. We must prioritize our lives and maintain balance.

We live in a fast-paced world where an actual phone call is becoming rare. Texts and e-mails are the norm, so when someone actually calls, I think it's an emergency. There are pros and cons to just about everything in life, but we must maintain our schedules. Too many times, we allow other people to control our day, and when we do, we and the ones we love the most end up paying the price, not everyone else. The others got what they wanted, but you didn't.

I served as a youth minister at a church in the Dallas, Texas, area for a while, and though I was there to teach and mentor, many times I was the one who learned the most. One particular afternoon, the father of an eighteen-year-old in our youth group rushed into my office unannounced and in a panic. He put his head between his hands and elbows on the desk and began to cry uncontrollably. Of all the members in our church, he was by far one of the most successful according to societal standards. He had a wonderful family, a huge home, a multi-million-dollar company, and anything else a person could ask for. Most importantly, he was humble, generous, and down-to-earth. He was one of those guys who seemed to have everything go his way. If he were entered in a car giveaway, he would win it. He was very happy go lucky and always maintained a positive demeanor. Needless to say, I was shocked that he of all people was crying in my office out of the blue.

"Hey, bro, what's wrong?" I asked.

"I'm sorry for barging in like this," he said. "I haven't slept in two days, and I don't know what to do."

"No problem, but what happened? Are your kids okay?"

"Don't worry—nothing's wrong necessarily," he said. "I just have the worst feeling of regret imaginable, and I don't know what to do about it."

"What do you regret?" I asked.

"Logan, my daughter, is my pride and joy. There's nothing on this planet I wouldn't do for her. Tomorrow she's graduating from high school—eighteen years old. Yesterday she was eight, and I missed it," he explained. "I would do anything to get that time back. I would do anything to see another recital or volleyball match. I never thought the time would go by so quickly. I look at all of the late work-related meetings I had and, thus, all of the kids' events that I didn't see. I would give away everything I have to start over and do it again!"

Time and time again we lose balance in our lives, and often it's too late before we realize it. Make sure you schedule time with your family, spouse, kids, and friends just as you do work-related meetings.

I'm as guilty as anyone. I schedule work meetings all day every day, but after that gentleman came into my church office, I started scheduling family meetings. My wife and I have Friday nights reserved for our date night. There may be only a couple Fridays in a year we miss our date night, and I will always make it up either the day before or after. The gentleman in my church taught me far more by rushing into my office than I could have ever taught him. That day literally changed my life. You see, we can get money back, but we can't get time back. There will always be meetings and work, but you have only one family. Cherish your schedule, and protect it more than just about anything else you have. Every time someone tells me, "I don't have time," I say, "You have the same exact amount of time each day as everyone else on the earth. It's how you choose to spend it." Most of us won't find the time to invest in our relationships, so we must *make* the time.

One of the best ways to find that extra time in your day is to multitask. For instance, I used to always struggle with my prayer time. When could I carve out time in the day to be alone with God? I devised the following solution: I run for an hour each morning (a perfect example of how the And 1 Principle adds up, as I used to run for only twenty minutes), so instead of listening to music, I pray as I run. As a result of this multitasking, I actually love to run now and have a much better quality of prayer time. I used to run to simply get and stay in shape. Now I get to have my alone time with God, too. Take a look at your day and see where you can possibly multitask to maximize your twenty-four-hour day, and then simply perform your maximized schedule the same way over and over again in order to achieve long-lasting results.

Repeatability

We've all heard the saying "Even a blind squirrel finds a nut every once in a while." Some people have a little success under this same premise, but I've never seen anyone have long-lasting success without the ability to repeat the proper success principles over and over. This skill is called repeatability.

What allows a professional athlete to keep his job? His ability to perform at a high level repeatedly. If a baseball player has one good game, he may get another chance, but if he can't repeat success, he will lose his job. I've served as an associate baseball scout for over a decade, and one of the key characteristics that scouts look for is repeatability. For example, in order for a pitcher to stay healthy and perform well, he needs a consistent arm slot. If his release point and arm slot are different from pitch to pitch, his location and command will vary from pitch to pitch as well. In other words, for my non–baseball fans, if the pitcher can't throw the ball and hit his spot consistently, he is not going to perform well.

Think about Olympic athletes. They practice the same exact thing over and over again in hopes of winning a gold medal once every four years. If that's not discipline, I don't know what is. They understand the importance of doing exactly the right things over and over again, as less than one-tenth of one second could be the difference between their years and years of training paying off or not. The ability to repeat every little facet of your life over and over again ultimately creates the positive habits you need to perform at the highest level day in and day out.

Commitment to personal development results in your ability to believe in yourself and have the vision and courage to take action on what you believe. It leads to the proper habits and the discipline to repeat the proper success principles over and over and positions you for the next step of success: the people business.

Chapter Summary:

1. What facets of your life need more discipline?
2. Where can you adopt the And 1 Principle?
3. Where do you need to be more consistent in conduct and conversation?
4. What distractions do you need to rid your life of?
5. Get out a piece of paper and a pen and write down your primary goal and action goals for all of the major facets of your life.

STAGE II of Success:
Building Teams

Chapter 5: Connect

Relational: to connect with all types of people anytime anywhere

There's a big difference between meeting with someone and building a relationship. Early in my career, a meeting had one primary goal: to reach the end result I'd come to the meeting hoping to acquire. For instance, maybe I wanted to close a business deal, sign a new player to one of the Dallas Patriots teams, or acquire new business. Perhaps the point of the meeting was to hire or fire an employee, deal with a difficult situation, or impress a coworker. Regardless, the meeting was simply a meeting with an end goal in mind. I was there to accomplish my agenda. Sometimes the meeting was a success and sometimes it wasn't, and though I hated meetings, I knew they were necessary. Then, one day, I realized that every meeting could be a successful meeting if I changed my entire outlook on the purpose of the meeting.

How great would it be if every time you went into a meeting, you left with more than you'd ever hoped to obtain? What if all meetings could be successes? Here's the good news: they can! When we move from speaking/listening to relational communication, we bring an entirely different mind-set to every personal encounter we have. In other words, be _relational_. One definition from Bing defines _relational_ as "involving relationship: involving or expressing a relationship." In other words, you are building a relationship with someone. When we truly engage in the relationship-building process, we don't simply communicate wants and desires; rather, we connect with the person we are with. The ability to connect with others opens you up to an endless network of friends, opportunities, ideas, and more. Every person you meet knows a lot of people who know a lot of people who know a lot of people. Therefore, walk into each meeting with the understanding that even if the person you are about to meet with is not the answer you are looking for, he or she can likely lead you to the answer. Moreover, you will have future needs and wants, and this person may bring value to a future endeavor. The bottom line: there are introducers and producers in just about every situation.

Introducers

Introducers basically connect people to other people. For example, a good friend of mine, Bill Clark (president of Louisville Slugger), was introduced to me by a mutual friend, Kevin Singleton. Kevin runs a great ministry out of New York, and I e-mailed him to congratulate him on his recent accomplishments and to inform him that I travel to New York frequently and would love to catch up with him. Long story short, Kevin e-mailed me back, one thing led to another, and Bill Clark and I have become good friends. Louisville Slugger is a partner with the Dallas Patriots, our select baseball organization, as a result of Kevin Singleton. The introducer, Kevin, led me to the producer, Bill Clark, which ultimately led to a successful partnership.

Producers

The producer is the one who makes the venture a success. In my case, I was hoping to have a great partnership with world-famous Louisville Slugger, and who better to make that happen than the president of the company, Bill Clark? The introducer sets things in motion, but the producer has the ability to actually make the deal happen. Every great organization has to have producers, and they are usually found via an introducer.

To be a success, it's extremely important to understand the significance of networking. Some of the greatest examples of networking can be found in social media. At the time of this writing, the 915 people I have as LinkedIn connections connect me to 9,988, 427-plus people, and over 72,635 people have joined my network in the past five days! Make sure you read that last sentence again, as I really want the power of networking to sink in. There's no way I, by myself, could know nearly ten million people, but through the power of networking, I have access to more than that just through my LinkedIn account. The best form of marketing is the relationship marketing method, a friend telling a friend. People would rather do business with people they know and trust than do business blindly. As a company, we never paid for any sort of advertising with the Dallas Patriots and Premier Baseball Academies for over a decade, and they became one of the largest baseball organizations in the country. Our customers had good experiences, so word of mouth spread, and the rest is history. We have introducers tell people all the time about the Dallas Patriots and Premier Baseball Academies, even ones who have zero affiliation with our programs! That's the power of networking.

In 2004, a friend of mine started a company in Dallas, Texas, that I was fortunate to be a part of. The company chose to use the relationship marketing approach to gather electricity and natural-gas customers. In our first few years in business, we were noted as one of the fastest-growing companies in business history, and we were the largest competitive retail electric provider in the state of Texas. A few years after that, we were noted as the largest competitive energy supplier in the United States. Again, networking works! Robert Kiyosaki was noted as saying, "The richest people in the world look for and build networks, everyone else looks for work."

Connectors

How do we build our network? We've discussed social media as a great tool, but the number-one way to build the best network is to connect with people. Let's be honest—if people were half as talented as their LinkedIn profiles suggest, we probably would have all heard about them by now! The only way to truly connect with someone is to build a genuine relationship in which the other person feels you care about his or her well-being. As we will discuss later in the book, *character* can be defined as doing things for someone else and expecting nothing in return. I've been extremely let down by a few individuals who stopped returning phone calls, texts, and e-mails once they got what they had been out to get. I truly cared about these individuals, and I even loaned one of them a lot of money when he was hurting financially. In fact, I gave this particular guy a cell phone. I found it ironic that he wouldn't return my phone calls or texts with the very phone I had given him. Time reveals people's true hearts, or lack thereof. Always remember to be real and genuinely serve the people in your life. Yes, you will be let down by some people, as I was. The sad reality is that those few people I described are still broke and struggling. They are no better today than they were years ago, and, most importantly, they've burned a lot of bridges. They have burned their introducers and producers. Here's the good news: for the few I opened my heart, resources, and time to who let me down, there are thousands upon thousands who have amazed me with their kindness and genuineness. The world has its bad people, but there is a majority of great people just waiting to connect. Connectors go into meetings looking to build a relationship. In other words, they want to connect with you and find common ground.

I'll be the first one to admit I fall short of this connection-oriented outlook at times. I'm a very type-A individual; thus, I really struggle with patience at times. Therefore, I oftentimes say a little prayer to remind myself why I'm meeting with a particular person or group. I'm meeting to *connect*! I'm meeting with them to add value to their lives and to get to know them. When you truly engage in connecting with others, you won't have to search far for partnerships, friends, and opportunities. You will have more than you have time for. As the saying goes, "Don't go out looking for friends. Go out to be a friend, and you will have an endless supply." Don't go out looking for great networkers, be a great networker. We will attract what we are! If we are friendly, we will have friends, and if we network, we will attract other networkers. Both enable us to increase our sphere of influence and, thus, our ability to be relational.

I once was invited to play in a golf tournament with a friend of mine I had met through an introducer. In this event, we played against another twosome. My first goal was to connect with the other two guys, as I didn't know them. Long story short, before the round was over, one had agreed to donate $5,000 to a charity I support. I had known the guy for only a couple of hours and we were there to play golf, not talk business, but every encounter with someone creates an opportunity to *connect*!

Once, as I was flying to Houston to speak to a group of more than one thousand business professionals, I overheard a guy on the plane next to me engaged in a stressful phone call with what sounded like his business partner. As the plane began to depart, he had to turn his phone off, but the last thing he said was "I need to find an attorney in Dallas quickly!" I engaged the man in conversation, and by the end of the flight, I knew the entire situation and, most importantly, his own personal struggles. He was finally headed home after weeks away on business, but I knew he needed to be at the event I was speaking at that night. His kids were growing up without him, and he hadn't connected with his wife in quite some time. His life needed a 180-degree turn. This man had been a complete stranger at first, but fifty-five minutes later, he jumped in a car *with me* and attended my speaking engagement that night. He didn't know me, but he knew I cared. He didn't know what I was going to be speaking about, but he knew I cared. He didn't know what I knew, but he knew I cared. Do you get it? When people know you care, you have connected!

One of my favorite examples of someone who moved from a "meeting" mind-set to a relational mind-set is a young man who went from financial struggle to financial freedom in the direct-sales world. He sent me an e-mail that read something like this: "I've given many presentations, but I can't get anyone to join my team. I need some help. Do you have any suggestions?" I've found this sort of sentiment to be rather commonplace in the world of direct sales. After attending one of my trainings, he realized he was making the common mistake of meeting with people without being relational. For people to move into action, they have to decide *they want to*, which usually means they realize they need to. If you are like this young man, my advice is simple: get to know what your prospects want out of life, and find out what's keeping them from reaching their goals. If you've ever heard me speak, you know that I usually tell the audience to ask themselves where they are at that moment (in terms of finances, relationships, time freedom, giving, etc.). Then, most importantly, I ask where they want to be (see the reflection questions included in the chapter 2 summary). If they could be anywhere, at any time, doing anything, with anyone, where would they be, whom would they be with, and what would they be doing? Now, what do we have to do to get you there? As the saying goes, "If you keep doing what you are doing, you are going to keep getting what you are getting—something has to change!"

What this young man was doing is very common: he was trying to sell his idea to his prospects. The bottom line is this: *no one wants to be sold things*. People want to make their own decisions on their own time—without pressure. Therefore, be a professional heartstring puller. In other words, if you can get to the hearts of your prospects and present your product or company as a solution to something in their lives, then they will make the choice to join you in your venture or buy your product because they see it as a solution to something they need or want to change. Until that paradigm shift happens, you are nothing more than a promoter of something. Be relational!

In my time as a youth minister, I had my share of meeting requests from parents with struggling kids. Some parents would sense a substance-abuse problem and ask for help. To parents' shock, I told them we couldn't help. I would explain that it was up to the person with the problem to help himself or herself. The youth ministry's job was to connect with individuals, make sure they knew we cared about them, and reveal to them the outcomes of the decisions they were making. If you are reading this and you've ever had to go to rehab or the like, you know exactly what I'm saying here. People with substance-abuse problems will change direction only when they decide in their hearts that they need help. A parent can check a kid into rehab, but that doesn't solve the problem. The transformation of the kid's heart solves the problem, and, yes, sometimes rehab can accomplish this goal. Dramatic change involves relational engagement of the heart!

Personality Types

In my opinion, there's no better way to connect with someone than to truly understand his or her personality type. We all have primary and secondary personality types, and they can change over time. No one personality type is better than another, but knowing people's personality types will help you connect with them and understand them better. While there are professional tests that can be done, such as the Myers-Briggs Type Indicator and others, I've adopted one that works for me based on a combination of tests. I did not invent what you are about to read; I simply adopted parts of it from friends and other studies from my career. The personality system I use is based on one simple fact: people want to be treated the way *they* want to be treated, *not the way you want* to be treated. Too often, we treat people the way we want to be treated, but that doesn't work, because a red wants to be treated like a red, not like a yellow, and so on. Below, you will find descriptions of the various personality types.

Red:

- is very direct and to the point
- has a type-A personality
- is focused on getting from point A to point B
- cares about details but doesn't want to deal with them
- needs other people to handle administrative details
- is a visionary leader, CEO type
- sees conflict as problem solving, not fighting or arguing
- is very impatient
- wants to be in control

To make reds happy, get to the point and add value.

Blue:

- is the life of the party and wants to have fun
- is direct in a fun and friendly way
- doesn't enjoy conflict
- typically makes a great salesperson
- is a great connector
- needs help getting started and staying focused at times
- feels that details aren't all that important
- dislikes structure

To make blues happy, make the process fun.

Green:

- is analytical
- feels that details are everything
- likes structure and systems
- is great at putting together spreadsheets and graphs
- is indirect but will embrace conflict to prove he or she is right
- typically makes a good accountant or attorney

- may struggle with paralysis by analysis

To make greens happy, tell them they are right.

Yellow:

- wants everyone to get along
- doesn't like conflict
- is very indirect
- is an incredible nurturer
- Is very patient
- sees the good in everyone

To make yellows happy, befriend them.

Let's use the car-buying experience to illustrate how the various personality types will go about their shopping experiences. The red will drive the car once and make a few calls to get the best deal or have someone make the calls for him or her. Then the red will be a pain in the rear for the car dealer when it comes to the negotiation. However, the negotiation doesn't have to be difficult if the car dealer knows how to identify and handle a red. Reds are actually a car dealer's best friends, because they are very decisive. In other words, reds want to be in and out the door as quickly as possible if the dealer is willing to save them time and money. But if a dealer tries to "sell" a red, the red will call the dealer out to his or her face and buy from someone else. Reds can't stand being told what to do.

When blues come onto a car lot, you can be certain they are going to want to take the fastest car on the lot for a spin. They want to see that baby go! Blues want to have fun, get the car guy's cell phone number, have a drink with him—you name it! Blues can be a car dealer's best friend or worst nightmare, because they will want to have fun and drive a lot of cars. Blues, however, will overpay for things. They care more about the experience than the details. If it's a great experience, the dealer has sold the blue. In this regard, blues contrast strongly with reds, who don't care about the experience and just want the quickest and best deal.

Greens will walk onto the car lot with more knowledge about the cars they are interested in than the owners and manufacturers of the cars! The key for the car dealer in this situation is to first understand that greens have done their homework and to then simply ooh and aah at how much the greens know, which allows greens to feel appreciated and validated based on their knowledge and understanding of the facts. The problem with greens in this example is the decision-making process. They will get paralysis by analysis, making the car-buying experience a *very long* process.

Yellow car buyers are the easiest and most enjoyable to work with, as they will overpay for anything if they feel that the dealer is their friend. I've learned this the hard way, as my wife is a yellow. My wife never even looks at the price, but you'd better believe she knows the person selling us whatever it is. In the case of buying a car, my wife once said, "I really like the person helping us, honey. He's so nice!" The red in me replied, "He's trying to break the record for the greatest amount of money one's ever spent above the asking price of a car!" My wife would rather overpay for a car to make the car salesman happy than engage in any type of negotiation. The moral of the story is this: if any of you reading this are dating or are married to a yellow, go with the person when he or she shops for anything of extreme value!

By this point, you either know your personality type or are greatly confused and need some guidance. Either way, it's important for all of us to know the personality types not only of others but also of ourselves. We all have weaknesses, and the more we know ourselves, the faster we can recognize those weaknesses. We can only fix our weaknesses once we know about them! Knowing I'm a red helps me understand how I come across to people. For those who don't know me, I can come across as arrogant, impatient, insensitive, and more. Being aware of how we are perceived is important! Remember, the goal is to be relational and connect with people. We all are guilty of jumping to conclusions about people. It's not a good thing, but it is what it is. Being aware of how we come across is vital to connecting with people.

Engagement

Success involves people, and the bigger your network, the more people you have access to. I'm commonly asked by those in sales how I engage in a conversation with people I don't know. The answer is pretty simple: people love to talk about themselves. Even the most introverted people will open up if you make the subject about them. Most people go wrong when attempting to connect with others by talking too much. Therefore, the first step in engaging in conversation is to ask questions. This can be with a person you know or with a total stranger, as was the case in the example of the guy sitting near me on the airplane. In addition to talking about themselves, people love to throw themselves parties—pity parties, that is. People love to complain! If you don't believe me, ask someone how his or her work is going. Few people actually like what they do—which is not a good thing—so, generally speaking, people love to complain. If asking about their jobs doesn't work—and I hope they do enjoy their work—then ask them if they have kids. People love to talk about their kids or family.

Next, be a great listener. Whatever you do, do not interrupt people when they are speaking. Remember, your job is to connect with them, so you must listen to everything they say in order to accomplish your goal. Make them feel special. You speak only when they are finished. If you can relate to something they said, do so briefly and then ask another question. Make the engagement about them, not you. If you are one of those people who is always trying to think of something to say while someone else is talking, *stop doing that*! It's hard to connect with people who behave that way. They come across as insincere know-it-alls who care only about themselves. Be a great listener. Make eye contact, be genuine, and care. I will be the first to admit that sometimes people ramble on and on and on, and the red in me wants to explode! I'll say the same to you as I say to myself: we are here to serve, not be served.

After you've asked questions and listened, it's time to relate. Assuming you asked plenty of questions and the other people engaged in the conversation, chances are you can relate to them. At this moment, you bridge the gap between them and you. By simply repeating what they've said, you can position yourself on their team. When they feel you are on their team, you have earned the right to exchange information. Congratulations, you have just expanded your network by who knows how many people! The three steps of engagement made me a multimillionaire in my twenties. It takes people to make things happen. The more qualified the people, the better your chances of success. As the saying goes, "Teamwork makes the dream work."

There are certainly exceptions, but in my time on this earth, I've been blessed to meet and know some of the most successful people in the world, and they are all great connectors. They understand the importance of relationships; recognize that some people serve as introducers, while others serve as producers; and realize that those roles change for a given person depending on the situation. To be relational is to truly understand people for who they are and treat them the way they wish to be treated. Through the power of engagement, your network can grow everywhere you go. Your next introducer or producer may come from your next trip to the grocery store. You never know!

Successful people value relationships. By being the best version of you, people will be attracted to you. As a relationship grows, trust is built and influence is earned. Influence is invaluable.

Chapter Summary:

1. Reflect on your mind-set when meeting with someone. Do you look to build a relationship or to simply get a result?

2. What introducers and producers can you reference from your life?

3. How do you need to improve as a connector to add more introducers and producers into your network?

4. What steps do you need to take to improve as a networker?

5. What's your personality type? What's your secondary color?

6. Write down a list of the top ten most important people in your life, and identify their personality types. Reflect on how you perceive them at times. Do their behaviors and actions make more sense when considered in relation to their personality types?

7. How can you use the four colors to help you in your career?

8. Using the three steps of engagement, start conversations with ten strangers over the next week and see how many you can successfully connect with. You will know you connected if you get their information.

Chapter 6: You've Earned the Right

Influence: the earned position in a relationship where people trust you in the decision-making process over an extended period of time

I've never met a person with influence who didn't value the relational component. The ability to build solid relationships must come first if you desire authentic influence. Before I go any further in this chapter, I must first debunk the biggest myth regarding influence. People often confuse a person's position with influence. For example, most individuals think the CEO or president of a company has influence over everyone else in the company. I disagree with this statement. CEOs and presidents have more decision-making opportunities, but that doesn't mean they have more influence. They do, however, have a bigger platform than most to establish influence. On the flip side, they have a bigger platform to ruin their influence as well. As the saying goes, "To whom much is given, much is required." We must not confuse a position with influence. John Maxwell, one of my favorite authors of all time and author of numerous *New York Times* best sellers, says in his book *The Five Levels of Leadership*, "Leadership is a process, not a position." In the case of position, people follow someone because they have to, but when people follow someone because they want to, that's influence! Put another way, your boss manages you, so you have to do what is asked of you, or you may lose your job. To a degree, this is certainly a form of influence, but for the sake of success, we need to see the term *influence* as an earned place in someone's life. Let's face it—if you force someone(s) to do something, the venture is not going to be nearly as successful as it would be if you got his or her buy-in. We all need to be careful about whom and what we allow to leave imprints on our minds. We are all very impressionable. *Be careful.* The shows and movies you watch, the music you listen to, the books and magazines you read, and the people you live life with make an impact on your life for better or worse! Because influence is so important, we must manage what our influencers are. For the sake of this book, we are using the term *influence* in a much stronger sense.

As we established in our chapter on being relational, people must first know you care if you want to reach their hearts. The process of building influence takes time because you must first establish a genuine relationship. Influence is a combination of three primary ingredients, and if you are missing even one of the three, you will be back at square one—being nothing more than a friend or acquaintance.

Relationship

Some sort of relationship must be in place before one moves to step two of influence. In the case of celebrities, they have influence because of their position—hence the reason they get paid so much to endorse products. Again, this isn't the type of influence I'm speaking of. I'm speaking of the type of influence that gets someone to follow your lead over an extended period of time. Truth be told, most of the celebrities you look up to would probably be huge let downs if you actually got to engage with them.

Trust

When a relationship matures over time, a bond is formed, and trust is earned. Once a level of trust is earned, influence begins to take place. The ability to trust people in today's world is rare, which makes those who are trustworthy an even more valuable commodity. I believe everyone wants to be great. Many people simply need help getting there. In other words, they need someone they can trust to show them the way!

Results

The greatest influencers I've ever known let their actions do the talking. The world is full of people who have all the answers but have no fruit. If a person is authentic, you will see the results. A friend of mine always says, "Beware of the naked man who offers you his shirt." Think about that for a second—doesn't make sense, does it? A naked man doesn't have a shirt. Exactly! There are a bunch of naked men offering their shirts (advice) who haven't earned the right to do so. If they know what they are doing, then why haven't they done it? Influence should be given only to those who have earned the right with their own personal examples in life. If other people offer you advice, take the meat and potatoes, and spit out the bones. In other words, don't discredit everything they are saying; try to learn something from them. However, don't take all advice as fact. Be guarded as to whom and what you allow to influence you. Remember, influence should have a track record if you are going to follow!

We've now covered the three primary necessities for influence: relationship, trust, and results. Influence is necessary if you want to be successful. Without it, you are powerless and left up to your own energies and efforts. With influence, you can build a team, and at that point, you can see the value of being the best version of you, when people follow your lead.

Teamwork

An absolute must for success is teamwork, and in order to establish teamwork, you must first establish a team. The best way to do so is through influence. The purpose of influence is to position you relationally to make an impact in what others do. Without influence, you are dependent upon yourself. With influence, you can engage others in your goals. As the saying goes, "Do you want to get paid on 100 percent of your own effort or 1 percent of one hundred people's efforts?" If we are getting paid only on our own efforts, we will never get ahead of those who leverage time by utilizing teamwork. The topic of teamwork is a book in and of itself, so suffice it to say that the principles of this book are to guide you in your team-building process. Taking ownership of yourself puts you in a position to mentor others to success, thus duplicating your efforts and leveraging time.

Mentor

After the relationship has been formed, the trust factor is solid, the person has a proven track record of success, and teams are being built, a mentor is more important than ever. Mentors can set the environment in place for others' success. Put another way, mentors guide and direct their protégés. Let's not confuse mentors with managers. Managers simply tell people what to do and not do. Managers may not have any relational tie to people other than the position they have, and they may have zero results. On the other hand, mentors empower people to ultimately spread their wings and fly—oftentimes further than the mentors ever have. Mentors have proven track records, are invested in and care for their protégés, and can be trusted. A mentor oftentimes is behind the scenes. A manager is always on guard. The mentor understands that the spotlight is on the protégé. The protégé understands he or she must be a great follower. The mentor has earned the right to lead, or else the protégé wouldn't have chosen the mentor.

If you are like me, you may be asking yourself, "Who can be my mentor?" Mentors may have to visit with you only a few times a year. Their role is to simply guide and direct you and keep you on track. They aren't necessarily involved with you day to day. They are at the next stage of life that you hope to get to. Put another way, they are a level above you. I've had a few mentors in my life, and some of them didn't even know they were my mentors until later. They were available, they cared for me, they could be trusted, and they had proven track records that no one could take away from them.

Model

The role of a model is similar to that of a mentor, but there is one major difference: the model is actively engaged and is not just guiding and directing but also showing you what to do. In other words, add everything a mentor does with a person who is in the trenches with you and you have your model! Models are a lot harder to find than mentors, but they are there! They are harder to find because, most the time, they have accomplished what they wanted to accomplish and have moved on to the next chapter in their lives. They no longer need to be in the trenches, so they aren't. If you ever find a model, consider it a blessing to have him or her in your midst, if even for a day. Be a sponge and soak up his or her knowledge! The reality is that most models probably won't be in the trenches for long, and if so, not with the same person. To reach the point of being mentors or models, people have to master the art of empowerment, which basically means they crank out successful people as fast as they can and then kick them out of the nest to spread their wings and fly. Great leaders work themselves out of jobs ASAP so that they can help others.

Within the modeling phase of influence, two important components take place: training and equipping. It's important to understand the difference. To train people is to teach them how to do something. To equip them is to give them the necessary equipment to succeed. For instance, I can train a baseball player for hours on how to hit a baseball, but until I give the player a bat, he will never have a chance to get a hit. The modeling process of success involves both training and equipping the protégé.

In my early twenties, I was blessed to meet one of the most successful team builders I've ever known. One of my good friends from high school called me one day while I was a baseball coach at Dallas Baptist University, with the intent of recruiting me into a business venture with him. He passed phases one and two of the influence quotient in that he was a friend of mine and I trusted him. He was successful at everything he did, so he passed stage three: results. The primary components of influence were good. The issue was that he and I were on the same level. He had influence with me, so I looked at his venture, but he wasn't in a position to mentor me, let alone model for me. As I discussed earlier, mentors are there to guide us to the next level. Someone on your level can't do that. What my buddy did next was one of the best success lessons I've learned; he had his mentor speak with me. I'll never forget the power this man had. He had built exactly what I wanted to build, and I'm not just speaking of a business. His family, lifestyle, wealth, and more were ideal. Most importantly, what he stood for in life was rock solid. I had the chance to see him speak publicly, and the message he gave that night in front of thousands of people sold me on the venture, and I was in from that day forward, and until the day he stepped down from his position. That one night led me to where I am today. I've made millions of dollars off of that particular industry because my friend was smart enough to get me in front of his mentor. Within a month, I passed my friend up and quickly became one of the top producers in the entire company. I was in my early twenties and made about $250,000 in my first year. Why? My friend had influence with me to get my attention and a mentor to move me into action!

The roles of the mentor and model are to do all that we've mentioned and one other very important thing: provide third-party credibility to your vision. To engage the best team possible, you may need someone a level above you to influence someone on your level to join your team or do business with you. Successful people understand the importance of surrounding themselves with people who have been where they wish to go, but that's sometimes easier said than done. Mentors and models provide the credibility to bring on the best talent.

Third-party credibility certainly played a role in the example I relayed about my friend; after the mentor's speech was over, I walked up and introduced myself after an introduction from my friend, and the rest is history. To this day, the mentor I'm referencing is one of my closest friends. Sometimes mentors lead masses rather than one person at a time. However, mentorship is a two-way street. Someone you admire is different than a mentor. For example, John Maxwell is an author I admire. Though I know him, he's not a mentor of mine, because he doesn't personally engage in that process with me. A mentor must be available and is a valuable part of your team.

Influence has served as an important factor in my success journey, and I'm grateful for the platforms I have to make an impact in people's lives. There's no way I would be where I am without great people around me. The purpose of influence is to make a difference in people's lives. If one abuses his or her influence, there will always be consequences, and the first is a loss of influence. It takes influence to build a team, and it takes a team to do great things. Personal development grows your platform of influence, and great substance protects your influence.

Chapter Summary:

1. The three stages of influence (relationship, trust, and results) are all needed. Which of these three areas do you need to work on?
2. Do you have a mentor and/or a model? If not, who in your life qualifies?

3. Do you both train and equip yourself and your team for success?
4. How has influence affected teamwork in your life?

Chapter 7: It's What Success Is Made Of

Substance: **what you are made of**

I love to study successful people, because even if I disagree with what they believe—or anything else, for that matter—they must have some substance. You can't reach high levels of success without consisting of something great. It takes a combination of ingredients to make a great recipe. If one ingredient is off or is expired, it will make the product taste bad. Substance matters!

When I googled the word *substance*, I found the following definition: "A particular kind of matter with uniform properties." We are all a "particular kind of matter," I suppose. Then I focused in on the "uniform properties" part of the definition. I googled the definition of the word *uniform* and got this: "Always the same, as in character or degree; unvarying. 2. Conforming to one principle, standard, or rule; consistent." The definition of the word *properties* is as follows: "A thing or things belonging to someone; possessions collectively." When we put all of these definitions together, we basically get the following: a subject that is always the same and consistent that belongs to a person. The question we are left with is this: What is the subject? The subject is going to be 100 percent dependent upon what you want it to be. If you want it to be success, as I'm assuming you do, then let's look at what characteristics protect the success formula.

It's one thing to have the belief, vision, courage, discipline, relational capacity, and influence to acquire success, but what protects these important characteristics? In other words, what keeps the great leaders on top? A saying we need to remind ourselves of regularly goes as follows: my fear for you is not that you will be successful; it's that you won't be able to handle the success. Imagine reaching the pinnacle and then not having the substance to stay there! It may take years and years to reach the top, but it only takes one slipup for everything to come crashing down.

Look no further than pro sports to highlight amazing careers that came crashing down because an athlete couldn't remain faithful to his spouse. Look at the billionaires who are now in prison for doing things illegally. There are more examples than I care to write about, so instead let's focus on what it takes to stay at your best.

Character

I truly believe it's not *what* is being said that is the most important but *who* is saying it. This goes back to the chapter on influence. In the book *Talent Is Never Enough*, John Maxwell says the following:

> Many people with talent make it into the limelight, but the ones who have neglected to develop strong character rarely stay there long. Why? Because people cannot climb beyond the limitations of their character. Talented people are sometimes tempted to take shortcuts. Character prevents that. Talented people may feel superior and expect special privileges. Character helps them to know better. Talented people are praised for what others see them build. Character builds what's inside them. Talented people have the potential to be difference makers. Character makes a difference in them. Talented people are often a gift to the world. Character protects that gift. (191)

Maxwell goes on to say the following:

> People are like icebergs. There's much more to them than meets the eye. When you look at an iceberg, only about 15 percent is visible—that's talent. The rest—their character—is below the surface, hidden. It's what they think and never share with others. It's what they do when no one is watching them. It's how

they react to terrible traffic and other everyday aggravations. It's how they handle failure—and success. The greater their talent is, the greater their need is for strong character "below the surface" to sustain them. If they are too "top heavy" with talent, then they are likely to get into trouble. (195)

For those of you who haven't read John Maxwell, perhaps his thoughts on character will encourage you to go out and purchase his books. It's important to understand we are all sinners and all fall short (Romans 3:23). No one is perfect. Just writing about this topic is difficult, thus the reason I keep quoting John Maxwell!

The googled definition of *character* is "The mental and moral qualities distinctive to an individual." The mental and moral qualities distinctive to successful people tend to be pretty common. They are the qualities that keep us on track with our value systems. As discussed in chapter 1, I feel it's important to be yourself. One of my favorite quotes, by Oscar Wilde, says, "Be yourself; everyone else is already taken."

We are all guilty from time to time of comparing ourselves to other people, but the truth is, we shouldn't. Our job is to be the best version of ourselves. When we are ourselves, we are comfortable in our own skin. In my personal experience, the search for self wasn't the easiest. When I decided to study my Maker, I realized a lot more about myself and what I was designed to do. When I tried to be what the world told me to be, I just felt deflated. For those of you reading this, it's critical you know your purpose for being on this earth. All the worldly possessions in the world won't make you joyful and at peace. There's only one cure for that, in my opinion, and that is to study your Maker. Even if you aren't a Christian, just read the Bible and see what happens to your life. Start with the book of Matthew and then Romans. I think you might enjoy it.

In the book *Next Generation Leader*, Andy Stanley says the following: "Your gifts will open doors. Your character will determine what you do when those doors have opened." We will all have moments to be great in life, but without character, we will miss those opportunities. Moreover, those opportunities will become few and far between. Your talent and character must be on the same page, because your talent will not be able to outpace your character for long. Andy Stanley says, "There is no cramming for a test of character. It always comes as a pop quiz. You're either ready or you're not. It is the law of the harvest at work. In the moment of testing, you will reap what you have sewn."

I can assure you I have failed many character pop quizzes in my lifetime. My goal is to never fail another one. We must pay close attention to how we think and what we value. If we don't, the world will bite us. The world screams at us every day to buy this, wear that, say this, and more. We must stay focused on what really matters.

We are all creatures of habit. Think about it. I bet you sleep on the same side of the bed every night. When you wake up, you probably have the same routine. The same is probably true for when you get ready for bed. If we aren't careful, we can form some bad habits. Substance—what you are made of—habits are more important than physical habits. If we focus on our inner being (substance), then those inner qualities will flow into our outer being. However, there are a lot of people who look incredible on the outside but are completely messed up on the inside. We see our outer being all of the time, which is the reason we buy nice clothes, work out, and do everything possible to look good. We don't see the mess we create on our inside; thus, we tend to neglect it. We must realize that the inside is where it all begins and ends. We must form the proper habits to build who we are at our core, just as we do our outer being, because our talents can't outpace our character.

Darren Hardy, the publisher of *Success* magazine and author of *The Compound Effect* (a book everyone should read), provides the following formula:

Small Smart Choices + Consistency + Time = Radical Difference

This is the same way our personal development works. How do you build character? Develop the proper habits, and rid yourself of the wrong ones. Nothing great happens over night. The formula is basically saying you must do the right things repeatedly over an extended period of time (discipline) if you want success. To have the right character, we must embrace the proper characteristics and values each and every day of our lives, repeatedly over an extended period of time, and in time, we will improve from the inside out. When we put the right things in, we push out the wrong things. In other words, we form the proper habits and rid ourselves of the bad ones. Remember, doing the wrong things repeatedly over an extended period of time has a compound effect as well!

Darren Hardy offers the following advice for breaking bad habits:.

> Look at your list of bad habits. For each one you've written down, identify what triggers it. Figure out what I call "The Big 4's"—the "who," the "what," the "where," and the "when" underlying each bad behavior.

Be aware of the who, what, where, and when moments in life—when you say something you shouldn't say, act in a way you shouldn't act, or engage in any other type of conduct that goes against the character you stand for. By identifying these triggers, you can eliminate them from your life if need be. Again, you become what you repeatedly do, and you become whom you hang around with. The habits you form and the people, places, and things you allow to enter your world can be a good or bad thing. Whatever we do, we must be men and women of the right substance if we ever wish to reach our God-given potential.

Influence takes time to earn, and it can vanish with only one mess-up. We've established the importance of influence if you want to build teams. The substance of the team is a reflection of its leader. Great teams have great leaders, and more often than not, they are leaders of substance.

To understand what it takes to build a team, we simply need to reflect on each chapter of this book. Each chapter consists of substance a leader must have or learn if he or she wants to be successful. In order to be a good leader, you are going to need good followers. If you want to be a *great* leader, you must have great followers. Within this group should be other great leaders. You will never have other great leaders if you yourself don't lead by example. The importance of substance has a compounding effect on your entire mission of success. In order to be great, you need others who are great, and you will attract great people only if you yourself have the character and substance to lead them. If you don't have the substance your team members deserve, they will leave and find a team that does.

I'm often asked how the Dallas Patriots grew so quickly into one of the largest and most successful baseball organizations in the country. My answer is always the same: by the blessing of God and the people we surround ourselves with. I'm one man who, in 1999, was blessed with a vision. My job was to carry out that vision. The number-one reason I am where I am today is because of who I am. I make plenty of mistakes, but I never stop challenging myself to be a better person and leader. I start every morning by reading a daily devotional and posting it to www.loganstout.com or my blog. I read the Word of God and pray each day. I'm always reading a personal-development book, such as the ones I've mentioned in this book. I truly believe in the saying "You don't know what you don't know." Therefore, I'm constantly trying to improve my substance. I know God will only bless me with the gifts I deserve. If I'm not the man He wants me to be, He won't trust me with more gifts. I must keep growing as a person and increasing my capacity as a leader if I want to be more successful and help others. The Dallas Patriots and Premier Baseball Academies have amazing people who are committed to growing as human beings. Our substance is rock solid; we bleed our mission statement and core values. Our mission statement is as follows: "Our mission is to Honor God, Strengthen the families mentally, spiritually, and physically, while providing the best baseball experience possible." Our core values are to always do what's best for the kid, both on and off the field; provide the best customer experience we can; and have a commitment to excellence in everything we do. Do we make mistakes as a company? Yes! Do we always apologize, ask for forgiveness, and make things right? Yes! I believe that as long as I continue to grow as a person and instill that same mind-set within our staff, the Dallas Patriots and Premier Baseball Academies will continue to be blessed and serve more and more people. This is the same challenge I want to relay to you as a leader. You don't have to be the leader of a company today. You must first be the leader of yourself. The more substance you have, the larger your platform will grow. It takes substance to handle the role of leading others, because as you grow, so does your responsibility. And the more responsibility you have, the more people you are responsible for. With more people come more problems. Substance drives us through the adversity of life in a godly, moral, and ethical way so that our success is not only continued but also improved!

Adversity

Character is an important part of substance, because as you grow, so will your adversity. Zig Ziglar said it best: "The higher you go, the stronger the wind blows." This is so true! Anyone who's had any major level of success has had people make stuff up about him or her, write crazy things on blogs—you name it. It's an unfortunate situation we live in, but people like bringing other people down. Typically speaking, people don't want to see others succeed without them. There are exceptions, and hopefully you are one of those people, but, generally speaking, the more successful you are, the more you are attacked. Attacks come from your enemies, the public, your opposition, the media, and more. Heck, just look at the church. If you are a megachurch, people are going to have some type of excuse as to why. The bottom line is this: adversity will strike, so let's look at some possible upsides of adversity.

In the book *The Upside of Adversity*, Os Hillman gives us six reasons for adversity:

1. To produce growth and maturation
2. To enable us to better understand and minister to others
3. To test us
4. To help prepare us for our calling in life
5. To leave our faith to God and not our own doing
6. To help us remove sin from our lives

If you stop and think about any adversity you've had in your own life, I bet the end result, after the smoke cleared, could be looked upon as a gift in one of these forms. Our biggest growth typically occurs during our biggest struggles. When life is great, it's easy to get complacent and put life on cruise control. It's also easy to get a little too confident. Adversity keeps us hungry.

The ability to relate to others is crucial to building relationships. Helping someone who is going through a tough time can best be done by a person who has been in a similar situation. When we go through difficult moments, we are tested, just as Job was tested. We need to rely on God during these moments and help others to do the same.

Success takes place with people. To deal with people, you must learn to deal with adversity. The more people there are involved in a venture, the more thoughts, opinions, and views are shared. Adversity in life prepares us for the blessings of leadership.

No one likes a wake-up call, but we all need one from time to time.

Adversity can serve this purpose. Sometimes sin sneaks up on us and surrounds us in ways we never imagined, and through adversity, the sin is brought to our attention. Adversity can be a great detour or yield sign to help us get back on track to avoid danger or simply slow down.

Too often we see adversity as solely negative. It's safe to say that adversity is generally not pleasurable, but that doesn't mean it's negative. If we embrace adversity as a positive and a learning opportunity, we are a lot less apt to make the same mistakes again. If we choose to sulk and wallow in our sorrows when adversity strikes, we are sure to make the same mistakes over and over. A person's substance will ultimately determine how he or she handles adversity. Moreover, the substance of a company will ultimately determine how the company handles adversity. Adversity is inevitable; it's how we handle it that determines our outcome.

We are all made up of what we allow ourselves to consume. If we consume the right mental values and morals, we will consist of the proper substance. If we don't, we aren't going to have the results we should. Our character enables us to lead ourselves and those around us in the ways we were intended to live, regardless of the curve balls life throws our way.

In addition to the key success characteristics I mention in this book and discuss regularly at www.loganstout.com, the following are the words and terms that I embrace in my journey toward having the best substance possible, and I truly feel they are fundamental to my substance quotient.

- **Accountability:** Those who keep me on track and tell me when I'm off provide accountability. We all need constructive feedback. We may not like what we hear, but we need to hear it anyway. The sad reality is that most people would rather be showered with praise and admiration than hear the truth. Praise and admiration can stunt our growth if they're not honest. The best way to grow is to hear constructive feedback and embrace it!
- **Honesty:** Always tell the truth regardless of whether it's good or bad. One of my weaknesses at times is exaggeration. I get excited during vision-building processes; thus, I may say what I truly feel is going to happen, but it hasn't happened yet. I'm

out of line in these cases. There's never a reason to exaggerate, as it's a form of dishonesty. Honesty is one of the most important traits people look for in a leader. If you lose the trust of your team, you lose your effectiveness as a leader!

- **Availability:** Always be available to those who matter to you most. I maintain a very busy lifestyle by choice. However, I'm never too busy to meet with those who have earned my time. Being a great listener shows you care. Being available is the best way to listen.

- **Accessibility:** The only time I can't be reached during a day is when I'm sleeping or on vacation. Every time you aren't accessible, you may have missed an opportunity that's gone to someone else. One of the number-one things I look for in hiring personnel is accessibility. One of my biggest pet peeves is people who aren't accessible.

- **Balance:** I've strategically placed balance after availability and accessibility. We all need balance in our lives, so we can't be accessible or available to everyone. For the people I know, I'm always a text, e-mail, or phone call away. Those I don't know have a way of reaching those who guard my schedule and time. The more successful you become, the more people pull on you for time. It's important for you to keep balance in your life, or you will end up giving less and less time to the most important people and things in your life. You can get money back, but you can't get time back. Guard your calendar. Everyone else thinks in terms of his or her time, and so should you! In the beginning of my career, I said yes to everyone. I finished each day exhausted. No one performs at his or her best without balance.

- **Dependability:** Do what you say you are going to do. I have always been a handshake guy. In other words, if I say I'm going to do something, I will do it. If for some reason something changes outside of my control, I will pick up the phone and make sure I communicate the change in plans. Too many people in today's world are flaky. You never know what you are going to get. Don't be that person.

- **Transparency:** I spend more time trying to figure people out than I do getting to know people sometimes. Live a life of transparency so that people know where you stand. When we have nothing to hide, life is a lot easier and we feel more freedom.

- **Loyalty:** A good friend of mine, former NBA Coach of the Year Del Harris, says in his book *On Point*, "Loyalty is deeper than trust. Loyalty denotes devotion and allegiance to a person, cause, or concept. Loyalty adds sentiment to trust" (78). Look no further than sports to see how loyalty has practically vanished from today's world. In the past, a player was proud to represent the organization he played for, and if the decision were left up to him, he would stay with that team his entire career. In today's world, players bounce from team to team. Everyone seems to think the grass is greener on the other side. If that's the case, then why do people keep jumping from team to team? The reason is that the grass is rarely greener on the other side. The grass is what you make of it. If you feed and nourish your grass, it will grow to be the greenest of all grass. We are teaching our kids the wrong message in how we value loyalty. Every situation in life will have ups and downs. Remain loyal to the cause, and fix the problems; don't run from them.

- **Attention to Detail:** I get the saying "Don't sweat the small stuff," but I don't agree with it. The small details in life lead to the big victories in life. If you can't handle the small stuff, how are you supposed to handle the big stuff? I agree that we need to focus on the big picture and not micromanage, but we need to pay attention to the small details. This is what separates the good teams from the great teams. Details matter.

- **Closure:** The more doors we leave open before we go to bed, the harder it is to sleep at night. I always aim for closure in any project, conversation, argument, or issue. There are people who never get closure, and I don't know how they function well. Maybe they don't. Confrontation is needed at times in order to create closure. Never be afraid to confront an issue as long as you do so in a peaceful way, with pure motives and intentions. When closure is reached, peace is restored.

- **Hunger:** In *Launching a Leadership Revolution*, authors Chris Brady and Orrin Woodward say the following:

  Hunger itself is one of the biggest facets of leadership. Hunger provides the stamina to persist, and the will to finish an endeavor. It is this hunger or ambition that births leadership. Leadership is not determined by one's birth, as they believed in Europe in the Middle Ages, nor is it determined by one's position, as many believe today; but rather it is determined by influence and performance. Hunger is its cause.

Reflect back on the accomplishments of your life. There was a substance deep down inside of you that spurred you into action in those cases—hunger!

- **Focus:** The very best know how to turn up their game when it counts. The thought of failure never enters their minds. They focus only on the idea of being a hero, and nothing clouds their mind-set in that moment.
- **Love:** When asked to summarize all of His life lessons, Jesus said, "The greatest of these is love" (1 Corinthians 13:13). Our world trains us to find fault in people. Heck, just read a tabloid. Tabloids pick apart people's clothing, hair, relationships, and more. I'm the first one to admit guilt here as well. We must remember that no one is better than anyone else. We are all equal, with unique talents and gifts. Our job is to find the good in people, not the faults. Love people, even your enemies. Love does no wrong.

As we reflect on the many substances we need to be the best possible version of ourselves—or, in other words, to be successful—there's one major component we haven't mentioned yet, and without it, we have nothing more than great ideas and notes. As with any knowledge gained, we must apply what we've learned and take action!

Chapter Summary:

1. What are your core values?
2. Do you have them written down so that you can regularly reflect on them? If not, take the time to write them down.

3. What's your accountability?
4. Do you embrace adversity?
5. List the most significant adverse moments of your life. Looking back, what were the blessings that came from those moments?
6. Make a list of the substance you need to add to your life. Which negatives do you need to remove?

Chapter 8: Play Ball!

Act: to create movement

The power of simply doing something creates an amazing result. I'm the first one to admit I don't necessarily like the process of writing a book, but I love to share my thoughts on success. I have a passion for helping people reach their God-given potential in life. How in the world was I going to write a book that could express my experiences, thoughts, and ideas if I didn't like writing? My answer was to sit down in front of the laptop and get after it! That's right—just start typing. Take action! Writing a book is no different from anything else we want to accomplish in life; we must start before we can ever finish.

I've often heard the saying "You won't regret the things you do in life nearly as much as the things you don't do." John Maxwell says the following in *The 15 Invaluable Laws of Growth*:

> We need to train ourselves to fight for positive changes. How do we do that? By remembering that our choices will lead to either the pain of self-discipline or the pain of regret. I'd rather live the pain of self-discipline and reap the positive rewards than live with the pain of regret, which is something that can create a deep and continual ache within us.

I've had the desire to write this book for a few years, but I never took action. I finally got sick and tired of talking about writing a book and said, "I must sit down and start if I ever plan to finish." What was it that got me to start in the first place? A burning desire to complete the vision. I knew it would be a challenge for me, but I'd rather live with the short-term challenge than the long-term regret of never writing the book.

Your Why

We must have a hunger that propels us forward into and through any endeavor. Let's face it—life can be difficult, and the bigger the challenge, the more obstacles and challenges you will face. Success is a result of a *why*, or hunger, that no one can take from you. If your *why* isn't big enough, chances are you will quit. Your *why* bridges the gap from the excited phase one of a task, through the valleys of struggle and discouragement, to the peak of accomplishment. Action depends on a strong enough *why* to not only start but also keep moving! My *why* for writing this book is an overriding passion to make an impact in people's lives—the two most important people being my two boys. I want to leave a legacy they can read and pass down to others that outlines what success truly looks like. Every time I look my boys in the eyes, the burning desire to write this book hits me at my core. Your *why* must do the same for you. I used to think motivation must happen for action to occur, and, to some extent, I still do. But after reading a great point by John Maxwell in *The 15 Invaluable Laws of Growth*, I see both sides. Maxwell writes,

> To do the right thing, I don't wait to feel like it. I recognize that emotion follows motion. Do the right thing and you feel right. Do the wrong thing and you feel bad. If you take control of your behavior, your emotions will fall into place.

Motivation and action work hand in hand. We may start a project because we are motivated to do so, but action motivates us even more.

Part of my morning routine is to go to the gym. There are some mornings when I simply am not motivated to go. But I go anyway (action). When I arrive at the gym, my motivation for working out tends to go up as I get into my workout. It isn't motivation that takes me to the gym in this example, because I'm not motivated. It is action that takes me to the gym, and my motivation increases afterward. One particular day, I planned to do only cardio. By the end of my workout, I ended up doing cardio, abs, weights, and sauna. The simple act of going to the gym motivated me to do more. Here's the best part: Because I felt so good, I got in better shape. By getting in better shape, I'm more motivated to keep going to the gym.

One of my biggest weaknesses is chips and queso. I'm motivated to stay in good shape, so I don't eat chips and queso often. However, when I take action and start eating chips and queso, I tend to eat the chips and queso for a long time! In other words, action can be a dangerous thing if it's the wrong kind of action. This is how habits are formed. Action leads to more action. Let's make sure we evaluate our actions so that we are creating positive actions in our lives, because negative actions create bad habits and results.

Activity versus Productivity

Activity and productivity are two very different things for successful people. I know plenty of people who seem to stay active but never seem to get anywhere. On the flip side, some of the most productive people I know aren't nearly as active as the nonproductive ones. When we take action, we must make sure it's leading us in the direction we desire to go. We should ask ourselves the following questions: Are my actions leading me to my final destination? Could my time be used in a better way? How can I delegate some of these tasks and focus my time on something bigger? These are common questions successful people challenge themselves with on a regular basis. Maximize your time. Utilize others to help you be more productive.

In the case of writing this book, it doesn't make sense for me to be the editor. First, I can use my time on other things. Secondly, I'm not nearly as productive as an editor when it comes to editing. We have time for only so many actions in a day, so choose your actions wisely.

As an eleven-year-old boy, I started my own lawn-mowing business in Richardson, Texas. With the help of my grandfather and stepdad, I managed to buy the equipment, construct a trailer to carry everything, and purchase a riding lawn mower so that I could drive everything from yard to yard. I had a really strong business at the time, especially for an eleven-year-old. The only problem I had was that I was a one-man band. In other words, the company worked only if I did. Though I was productive, my time wasn't spent to the fullest. So I "hired" some help. My brother and some of my other friends wanted to make some extra money, so I put them to work. I was able to double the amount of yards I had and spend a lot less time actually doing the work. At an early age, I learned the importance of leveraging resources and maximizing time. When I did all of the work myself, I was a lot more active but a lot less productive. In the end, I was a lot less active, a lot more productive, and a lot more profitable, but, most importantly, I had more time freedom! Check your activity-versus-productivity scale.

Mind-Set

Thinking is an action—an important and never-ending action. Successful people learn to control their thoughts. Your mind is going to be thinking whether you want it to or not, so why not control it?

One of the biggest obstacles I had to overcome—and still struggle with at times—is negative assumptions. I always start to think of the worst possible scenarios when something isn't going the way I hoped it would. I think we can all be guilty of this to an extent. For instance, have you ever called someone who didn't return your phone call? Then perhaps you sent a follow-up e-mail or text, and the person didn't reply to those either. My first thought used to be, *What did I do wrong? Is he mad at me or something?* As it turned out, perhaps the person was out of the country. It was no big deal, but you stewed on the issue for days or even longer, worried about why you hadn't heard back. We must control our thoughts.

In the book *Positive Intelligence*, author Shirzad Chamine says the following:

> High Positive Intelligence means your mind acts as your friend far more than as your enemy. Low Positive Intelligence is the reverse. Positive Intelligence is therefore an indication of the control you have over your own mind and how well your mind acts in your best interest. It should be relatively easy to see how your level of Positive Intelligence determines how much of your true potential you actually achieve.
>
> How often is your mind working against you? Positive Intelligence is a great action to add to your daily routine. Are your

thoughts simply active, or are they also productive? Remember, thinking is an action that must be valued and evaluated!

One of the key components to being successful in baseball is the mental game. You are going to fail more times than not in baseball, so you'd better be able to handle it. Think about it: you can fail over 70 percent of the time as a major-league baseball player and still make the All-Star team and Hall of Fame. One coaching tool my staff and I use with our Dallas Patriots players is positive talk. In other words, we don't tell our pitcher, "Don't walk him." We instead tell our pitcher what we hope to accomplish: "Get your ground ball," or "Hit your spot." What we say out loud and to ourselves controls our thoughts more than we think.

Here's a quick exercise to illustrate this point. Really focus on what I'm about to ask you to do. Here we go:

> Do not think about a black-spotted cow. Whatever you do, do not picture or think about a black-spotted cow.
> What did you just think about? A black-spotted cow!

Try this one:

> Do not think about an airplane. Don't think about the airplane!
> You see, when we tell ourselves to not do something, we are working against the very goal we are trying to accomplish. Think about what you want to do. As a player, my greatest strength was my mind-set. As a hitter, my thought process was simple: see ball; hit ball. I wanted to hit, and I knew I was going to hit. Whenever I went into a slump, it was typically a problem with my mind-set. I wasn't thinking successfully; thus, I struggled. That's how life works. When our mind is right, we perform correctly. We must make sure the actions of our minds are in harmony with what we want out of life.

My rule of thumb is simple: when things start to speed up or get out of control, step back, assess the situation, evaluate the best course of action, and then take action. At no time does panicking or relying on luck of the draw make sense. When we step back, assess, and evaluate, we take the emotion out of a situation—to the best of our ability—and use reason. We gain control of our mind-set. The ability to control the mind keeps our eye on the target so that we can reach our desired result.

Dream Big

Dreams are nothing more than a series of thoughts. Dreams are a part of our mind-set, and like thoughts, they can be productive. It's important we never limit our imagination. Successful people look for ways to make things work while everyone else finds reasons why something won't work. It takes the same amount of effort to dream small as it takes to dream big, so why not dream big?

I have a great family, but I didn't exactly grow up in an ideal situation. My parents divorced when I was very young, so my mom did her best to raise my younger brother and me. We had an apartment for a while, and then, with the help of her parents, we were able to move to a better part of town. Like most people in the world, she was in survival mode—meaning that she pushed her dreams way back, as figuring out how to pay the bills each month was her primary focus. She supported me in my endeavors but never really pushed me into any one thing. Again, she was simply hanging on. She remarried after a while to my stepdad, Gary. He is one of the most amazing people I've ever known. He was the perfect stepdad. He never tried to be my dad but was always there when I needed him. My mom's dad—Pete, as I called him—was the man in my life who taught me work ethic and business. He was truly a man's man. He passed away in November of 2011, but I will never forget him. He taught me what it meant to be a great parent, friend, husband, and more. I wouldn't be where I am today without him. My dad, however, is the dreamer in the family. He was always the one telling me I could be anything I wanted to be. Heck, he's the one guy who still thinks I could be playing a pro sport even now—because I know I couldn't!

Just about every weekend I can recall, my dad was working on his dream. He had his own setbacks in life, as his first career came to a screeching halt. He was a pioneer in the scuba-diving world, living his dream, until the time came when he couldn't make a living doing it anymore. He had to completely change careers and go back to school during what should have been the prime of his career. Put another way, he had to start dreaming again. I still remember watching him study around the circular wooden table in his apartment every day and night. On the weekends we went to his apartment, he apologized about his studies but always said it would be the best thing for all of us in the long run. While most kids were out playing, my little brother and I sat in an apartment, watching TV or coming up with any creative game we could play to pass the time. We didn't fully understand what our dad was up to, but we knew life had thrown him a curve ball and he was doing everything in his power to knock it out of the park. To this day, my dad shares his dreams with whoever will listen. When my wife, Haley, and I take my dad to dinner, the topic of his next book, business idea, and more always comes up. My brother and I laugh about it fairly regularly, but that's what kids do, right? They make fun of their parents! The truth is, my dad always dreams big. Ultimately, he got his degrees and an amazing job. My brother and I were in high school by that time, so it took awhile, but my dad did it. He dreamed big and, as a result, was living the life. He had tickets to every major event you could imagine, a great house, nice cars, and a huge salary. He was doing well. To this day, my dad accomplishes dreams most only think about. He's an author and college professor. He put his dreams to the test and paid the price, and he's seen the fruit. My dad taught me with both his words and actions to dream big. I'm forever grateful to my dad for his dreaming, as it rubbed off on me. The world is full of dream stealers. Be a dream maker for yourself and for others. Be like my dad—help people dream big!

One of the most important things I've learned in working with people is the bigger your dreams, the better the people you will need to make the dream a reality. Big dreams aren't accomplished by yourself. They succeed like any other success; teamwork. When you start your dream process always remember the best dreams involve leaving a legacy.

Success versus Significance

Selfish actions and legacy actions take the same amount of time, so why not pursue something that makes an impact in the world? Success is reaching your God-given potential in life. Significance is helping others do the same. Pastor and radio broadcaster Tony Evans says the following: "If you want a better world, composed of better nations, inhabited by better states, filled with better counties, made up of better churches, populated by better families, then you'll have to start by becoming a better person." I believe the greatest way to make an impact in the world is to help people be the best versions of themselves. I wrote this book to help people understand how to be successful with the purpose of passing on these ideas to others. What good is it to make a bunch of money and be lonely? Compensation doesn't merely come from what you are paid in money. The best forms of compensation are time, experience, knowledge, wisdom, and resources. When you take action, do so with the intent of making an impact. Our tiny amount of time on the earth should be spent adding value. Let's do everything we can to leave the world better than it was when we entered it. When your time is up, no one is going to care about your money or material possessions except those inheriting them. However, everyone you interacted with will remember who you were and what you stood for in life. What do you want people to say and think?

Some of you reading this book may think it's too late. In the words of Alan Cohen, "To grow, you must be willing to let your present future be totally unlike your past. Your history is not your destiny." Consider your life one big book. Remember, we can't change the previous pages of the book; the ink is dry. The good news is that we have a bunch of blank pages staring us in the face, and we have the choice to write them as we wish! Let's not allow our past to dictate our future. Successful people learn from the past but focus day by day and never lose sight of the big picture.

We've all known people who try to live off past successes. Isn't it miserable to watch? If you are in the boat where your past was great, congratulations! Now, what you are going to do with your future? How are you going to go from success to significance? God doesn't put us on the earth to simply exist; He wants us to thrive!

I sort of retired by the age of thirty. I say "sort of" because I'll never be able to retire. I'm a busybody. During my retirement attempt, I played golf six days a week and sometimes thirty-six holes a day. After about two months of this lifestyle, I became miserable. Every time I played golf, I felt as if I were wasting my God-given abilities. I had to do something more! I had received great financial compensation for all of my hard work over the years, but I was yearning for the compensation of giving back. This is the difference between success and significance. In other words, we are called to leave a legacy.

The Greatest Legacy

The greatest team builder and networker the world has ever known is Jesus Christ. Whether you are a Christian or not, I encourage you to learn from His life story. Even if you don't believe in Jesus, the story itself is amazing. Let's look at the facts. The Bible is the best-selling book of all time, and the story of Jesus Christ's death and resurrection on the cross is the one thing that truly separates Christianity from every other religion. I am a devout Christian, but for those who aren't, no one can deny that the story of Jesus Christ is the greatest movement in the history of mankind. No other movement in history even comes close to Christianity in regard to the duration or number of followers. In other words, even if you don't believe, I love you regardless, and I encourage you to learn from His example.

The life of Jesus involved a never-ending belief in His purpose for being on the earth. His love of His Father in Heaven was unwavering at all times. Jesus never once got off track. He lived thirty-three and a half years on the earth as a sinless man. He wasn't a man with great credibility or privilege. Rather, He was born in a manger and became a humble carpenter. God gave Him the vision to transform the world, and nothing stood in the way of that vision. He was to die on the cross for the sins of mankind and to build a team of people who would spread the news.

Jesus was the greatest team builder and networker the world has ever known. He didn't use flashy signs or commercials. Instead, He used the old-fashioned word-of-mouth approach: relationship marketing. He mentored twelve men. These twelve men weren't special. In fact, they were known for being the opposite. Jesus loved them anyway. He saw the greatness in those twelve men, while everyone else focused on their weaknesses. Jesus believed in people.

Jesus had more courage than anyone ever has. He knew the price He would pay for the decisions He made, but He carried through with His Father's plan anyway. Why? Because it was the right thing to do.

Great leaders make difficult correct decisions even when they know the majority will only find fault. Leadership involves the courage to stay humble and never complain and press onward despite all adversity.

The adversity Jesus faced was so strong that one might ask how His followers not only stayed with Him but also kept growing in numbers. He was relational, a man of substance. He broke bread with the least of us. He cared for the sick. Jesus earned influence. He didn't use fancy wording. He said, "Come, follow me" (Matthew 4:19; Mark 1:17). He was a perfect mix of red, blue, yellow, and green personality types. No one could question His character and integrity, as He was above reproach. Why, then, were so many against Him? Every great leader will have many who are against him or her. It's the price of leadership. Did Jesus care? No.

Jesus dreamed big; He knew of no limits. After all, He was a man of significance. He left a legacy. Anyone can find success, but few find significance. He came to serve, not be served. Through the power of building genuine relationships with those whom society considered to be the lowest of the low, He created the greatest movement the world will ever know: Christianity. Amen!

Chapter Summary:

1. What were your dreams in your youth? Is it too late to accomplish them?
2. What dreams can you put to the test? What sacrifices will you need to make to accomplish your dreams?
3. What is your *why(s)*?
4. Gauge your activity versus productivity.
5. What changes to your mind-set do you need to make?
6. What do you know you want to do but just need to take action to get started?
7. Do your dreams lead to success or significance? Why not both?
8. Dive into the life of Jesus to learn from the greatest legacy maker and success story of all time!

Closing

It's been a pleasure to share my life with you through the words of this book. My greatest strength is certainly not the written word. My accountability partners tell me I'm at my best in front of a group of people. If you would like for me to speak to or train your company or group, please e-mail my team at info@loganstout.com, and we will be in touch as soon as possible. Please email as at the same address as above if you would like to order a large volume of these books. I pray you will share this book with as many as your heart desires. The information written has changed my life, and I pray it changes yours. I look forward to connecting with you in the near future. Thank you, and God bless!

Bibliography

Brady, Chris, and Orin Woodward. *Launching a Leadership Revolution.* New York, NY: Hachette Book Group, 2005.

Chamine, Shirzad. *Positive Intelligence.* Austin, TX: Greenleaf Book Group Press, 2012.

Collins, Jim. *Good to Great.* New York, NY: Harper Collins, 2001.

Frankl, Victor E. *Man's Search for* Meaning. Vienna, Austria: Beacon Press, 1946.

Gallo, Carmine. *The Apple Experience.* New York, NY: The McGraw-Hill Companies, 2012.

Hagee, John. *The Seven Secrets.* Lake Mary, FL: Charisma House, 2004.

Hardy, Darren. *The Compound Effect.* Lake Dallas, TX: Success Books, 2010.

Harris, Del. *On Point.* Charleston, SC: Advantage Media Group Inc., 2012.

Hillman, Os. *The Upside of Adversity.* Ventura, CA: Regal Books, 2006.

Maxwell, John C. *The 15 Invaluable Laws of Growth.* New York, NY: Hachette Book Group, 2012.

Maxwell, John C. *Talent Is Never Enough.* Nashville, TN: Thomas Nelson Inc., 2007.

Stanley, Andy. *Next Generation Leader.* New York, NY: Multnomah Books, 2003.

About the Author

Logan Stout is a lifelong entrepreneur, former professional athlete and 17-time World Series player and coach. His accomplishments as a successful business leader, coach, motivational speaker and author stem from a desire to break down barriers that stand between people and the things that they want most in life.

His most recent business venture is directed in the area of health and wellness. Since its' launch in May 2014, IDLife, LLC has grown exponentially with partners such as Troy Aikman, celebrity trainer Jen Widerstrom and billionaire Darwin Deason. They are joined by nationally recognized authors and fitness ambassadors, as well as motivational speaker and leadership mentor, Keith Craft, on a journey to educate people on the importance of health and wellness and to provide the highest quality nutritional products.

He has also partnered personally with motivational speaker and Inc. Magazine's "Most Popular Leadership Expert in the World", John C. Maxwell, to bring leadership and personal development training to all 196 nations in the world.

Logan is also the founder and CEO of the Dallas Patriots baseball organization, where he focuses on mentoring and leading youth. This organization is now one of the largest in the world, providing select teams ages 6-18 years old with world-class instructors, coaches, training and mentoring. Every graduate of the Dallas Patriots baseball organization has earned the opportunity to play college baseball and many are MLB draft picks each year.

He regularly makes appearances on television, radio and at live events. He has been featured in numerous publications such as Philadelphia Life Magazine, The Dallas Morning News, The New York Times and numerous print and live media outlets. He has been on CBS Radio, The Fan, The Ticket, FOX and was named "Man of the Year" by Philadelphia Life Magazine

Logan Stout and his wife, Haley, have two sons and reside in Frisco, Texas. They are patrons and honorary chairs of the Boys and Girls Club of Collin County, the American Heart Association of North Texas and other charitable organizations.